COMF
GRAI

GU00363266

John Lansdown is an internationally recognised computing expert who has specialised in computer graphics since the 1960s. He has created the graphics effects for three feature films and over 100 TV advertisements and documentaries, and has held lecturing posts at the Royal College of Art and St Martins School of Art, London. He is currently Chairman of System Simulation Ltd in London.

TEACH YOURSELF BOOKS

COMPUTER GRAPHICS

John Lansdown

TEACH YOURSELF BOOKS

Hodder and Stoughton

ensures that any input, output, computation and storage is carried out in a correct and orderly fashion. In many personal computers, the operating system often tends to be a fairly simple item of software, limited in scope and allowing perhaps only the listing, saving, recalling and running of programs. In many professional machines (particularly those that support many users at once), the operating system is often extremely sophisticated and is sometimes the largest program the machine has to obey.

The language system

The language system allows us to create programs reasonably quickly and easily by permitting program writing in a style somewhat closer to human language than the abstract code used by the computer itself. Many personal computers support only one programming language – namely BASIC. Others, especially professional machines, have systems which can cope with a number of languages of which Fortran, Pascal and C are probably the most common for scientific and graphic purposes.

Limitations of standard programming languages

The basic units of hardware and software just described are usually provided by manufacturers as general-purpose graphics packages; purchasers are expected to employ these to write application programs to suit their individual needs. As none of the well-known computer languages were originally designed for graphics, manufacturers often supply versions of the languages enhanced to include appropriate graphics commands such as DRAW, MOVETO, CIRCLE and so on. Understandably though, as manufacturers wish to exploit the special features of their own machines, there is very little standardisation in these enhancements. As a rule, therefore, graphics programs written for one type of machine cannot be run on other types of machine without modification. This lack of standardisation not only makes program portability difficult to achieve but also presents problems in books such as this where, in order not to be too abstract, instructions have inevitably to be orientated towards particular machines and languages. We have attempted, however, to make our examples as general as possible. Urgent moves are afoot in the computer industry to bring about a measure of standardisation – at least in the sorts of graphic facilities provided. However, these efforts are likely to take a little time to influence the production of machines and programming languages. We have attempted to anticipate the acceptance of graphics standards by creating our programming examples roughly within the framework of current thinking in this area.

It is essential to realise that all the elements in a system are important and that defects in any one of these will limit the performance of the whole. The quality and types of drawings that can be created and the degree of graphical interaction possible depends on the available hardware and software. The extent to which you can properly exploit the full potential of the system depends on the quality and comprehensiveness of the documentation.

Graphic styles

Different types of system and, particularly, different forms of output device give rise to three different computer graphic styles:

1 Character or mosaic graphics.
2 Calligraphic or vector graphics.
3 Raster or pixel graphics.

Character or mosaic graphics

Here, as in Figure 2.4, drawings are assembled mosaic-fashion from a special set of graphics characters either supplied with the machine or designed by the users themselves. The characters are accessed

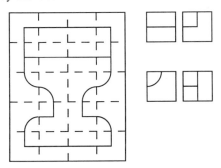

Figure 2.4 Mosaic type drawing showing four elements used

from the keyboard as if they were alphanumerics. With careful
design and ingenuity, some interesting pictures can be made in this
way, but drawing with characters is a very limiting style suitable only
to such things as simple diagrams, videotext and video-game
figures. Some personal computers can draw only in character
graphics.

Calligraphic or vector graphics

Here, drawings are made up from lines (often just in one colour).
This style, which is the one most often used for plotting onto paper,
can produce very accurate and complex drawings and is generally
the one favoured for engineering and drafting applications. It is not
easy to produce areas of solid colour by vector graphics, so this sytle
is not used when shaded drawing or a high degree of realism is
sought. VDU vector systems are expensive to produce hence,
except when plotting on paper, personal computers do not use the
calligraphic style.

Raster or pixel graphics

In this case, drawings are made up of arrays of closely-spaced dots,
called *pixels* (short for 'picture elements'), which allow either lines
or areas to be delineated in various colours. Because of the hardware simplification raster graphics makes possible, this style is
rapidly becoming the most widespread, but the dotted nature of the
drawings creates problems of accuracy and resolution which have
to be specially dealt with by software (or, sometimes, hardware)
techniques. The most visible manifestation of these problems is
that diagonal lines have a 'staircased' appearance which can be
disturbing. Most personal computer systems use this style of
drawing.

   In general, only vector and raster graphics are dealt with in this
book.

Graphic tasks

We use graphic systems in order to facilitate graphical input and
output. For input, we need support for three tasks:

1   Interaction with the system.
2   Setting-up and editing drawings and graphic text.

3 Converting existing drawings into machine form: a process known as *digitising*.

For output, we need support for two tasks:

1 Making drawings.
2 Creating graphical menus or symbols to assist in interaction.

Except in the case of some expensive equipment where special processors are incorporated, graphics computers differ from general purpose ones in respect of their input and output devices and the way these are supported by the software. For most applications, input and output are of equal importance, but it is probably true to say that those who sell graphics systems tend to stress only the quality of the output facilities of their product. Of course, an impressive output can only be demonstrated if the system is capable of providing it so, in that sense, the salespersons are not being misleading. Users soon find, however, that properly designed input facilities which are well-supported by comprehensive software are just as important if the graphics potential of the system is to be exploited to the full.

Graphics primitives

In order to allow us to carry out graphics tasks, systems come equipped with their own particular sets of drawing instructions, or *primitives* as they are sometimes called. Some systems, especially the more expensive ones, have comprehensive sets consisting of dozens of primitives to draw such things as lines, polygons, circles, arcs and other figures; to change line styles; to fill-in areas with solid colours or hatching; to erase or display portions of a drawing; to rotate, move or reflect figures, and so on – all with single commands. Other systems have much more limited sets of primitives, perhaps allowing the display only of single lines in one style and colour. Systems differ not only on the output tasks they facilitate but on the input tasks too; some will have no special input primitives, others will cater for input from all sorts of sources.

  To assist us in dealing with these differing capabilities, we will assume that the system we use has only six primitives: one to tell the system that we want to use graphics, four for output and one for input. We assume that the (x, y) coordinates given to the primitives lie within the ranges permitted by our drawing surface (Figure 2.5). Anything outside these ranges will give rise to an error condition. Our primitives are:

1   **GRAPHICS(n),** which clears the screen and puts the system into graphics mode if n = 1 and out of it (without clearing the screen) if n = 0. Any graphics instructions used when n = 0 (or if n is undefined) are ignored.
2   **MOVE(x, y),** which puts the drawing head (electronic beam or pen) in the position on the drawing surface defined by the coordinates (x, y) without making any mark or trace.
3   **DRAW(x, y),** which moves the drawing head from its present position, wherever that is, to a new position (x, y) leaving its own version of a straight line as it goes.
4   **TEXT(x, y, message),** which prints the string defined in message starting at point (x, y).
5   **COLOUR(n),** which sets the drawing colour to the hue (n). When n = 0, the colour is set to the same as that of the background so that anything drawn is effectively invisible. The object of having COLOUR(0) is to allow us to erase existing lines by drawing over them with the background colour.
6   **ACCEPT(flag, x, y),** which will take a pair of (x, y) coordinates from an input device and set the flag parameter to a number depending on some action performed by the user (such as pressing a button).

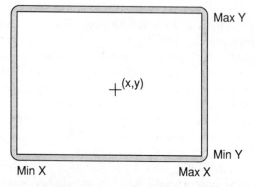

Figure 2.5   All points must lie within the drawing surface (i.e. in the range Min X, Max X horizontally and Min Y, Max Y vertically)

Thus, in our system, we can draw a triangle starting at point (15,30) with other vertices at (120,17) and (60,50) by using the instructions:

```
GRAPHICS(1)
COLOUR (1)
MOVE(15,20)
DRAW(120,17)
DRAW(60,50)
DRAW(15,20)
```

These will produce a drawing like that shown in Figure 2.6.

It is, of course, unlikely that your system will have precisely the set of primitives given above. It will, however, have equivalents. You will have to substitute the particular instructions your system permits before you can make use of any of the subroutines given in this book. Apple II owners using BASIC, for instance, will need to use something like the following to draw the triangle:

```
100 HGR
110 HCOLOR = 1
120 HPLOT 15,20 TO 120,17 TO 60,50 TO 15,20
```

(In fact, because of the way the Apple II defines its coordinate system, these instructions will draw the triangle upside down when compared with Figure 2.6.) The Apple II can draw lines in any of seven colours, so HCOLOR could be set to any number in the range 1–7 according to choice.

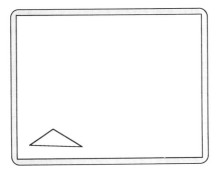

Figure 2.6 Triangle on screen

Our plan is to use our primitives to build up a more comprehensive set of instructions resembling those in a professional graphics system.

Exercises

2.1 Make a list of the graphics primitives of your system and check this against the one we give. You will probably have more items on your list but ensure that you carefully note the equivalents to ours. Keep this list for further reference because you will have to use your primitives in place of ours in order to produce drawings.

2.2 Using your primitives, try programming the triangle example and compare the output with Figure 2.6. Can the figure be recognised as a triangle or is it too small to be properly formed? Try it in various sizes and see what happens if you use real numbers rather than integers.

2.3 Is the origin (0,0) on your output device in the lower left hand corner, in the top left hand, or elsewhere? If it is fixed in the top left hand corner how can you ensure that your drawings are not produced upside-down? Hint: what happens if you subtract all the vertical dimensions in the drawing from the maximum vertical dimension of the screen?

2.4 What happens if you ask your system to draw a sloping line whose end points are outside the boundaries of the drawing surface? Does the system object to this, scramble the line in some way, or draw as much of it as it can? What happens is important, so experiment with different conditions until you know exactly the effect produced.

3

Input Tasks and Devices

The type of input facilities required depends to a large degree on whether the need is for *interactive* graphics – where the input tasks are carried out on-line with immediate visual feedback, or for *non-interactive* graphics – where the input tasks are dealt with as an off-line process separated from output. In the last chapter, we pointed out that the three roles of input devices are interaction, drawing creation and digitising but, of course, in the non-interactive case, the first role is dispensed with (as is the hardware to facilitate it). In both cases, the essential purpose of a graphical input device is to accept information and send it to the processing unit. In the non-interactive case this information usually represents nothing more than a description of the drawing (or *graphics object* as we will sometimes call it) to be displayed. On the other hand, in the interactive case, the information can represent not just graphics objects but a number of other things the precise nature of which the processor has to interpret according to context. It must then immediately display the result on an output device in order to give users direct visual confirmation that their instructions have been correctly carried out.

   Such interaction is greatly facilitated by use of a *menu*. This is an area either of the screen or of the work surface of an input device which is temporarily or permanently set aside for a list of elements. These elements might be commands such as DRAW, MOVE, ROTATE and so on, or graphics objects such as symbols representing tables, chairs and electronic components. In some systems, notably the Apple Lisa and Macintosh computers, the menu symbols are pictorial but they represent tasks or concepts rather than the real objects they depict. When they are used in this way, the symbols are known as *icons* and a typical icon might be a waste-paper basket to represent the task of disposing of some work, a filing cabinet to represent the action of storing information, or a pot of glue to represent the action of pasting one piece of drawing over another. If, by using one of the devices and methods dealt with in this chapter, the user chooses an item from the menu, the processor either performs the command or allows the user to work with the chosen graphics object.

Graphical input devices

The computing industry has recognised the variety and complexity of the input tasks that graphics users might need to perform and, in addition to the keyboard, has provided a number of different devices to aid the process. These include:

1 Light pens.
2 The mouse.
3 Joysticks, trackballs and thumbwheels.
4 Touchpanels and touchpads.
5 Knobs, dials and sliders.
6 Keys and function buttons.
7 Tablets and digitisers.
8 Scanners and line followers.

The devices vary in method of use, availability and cost. Some are very good at one or, perhaps, two of the basic input tasks but only a few can properly carry out all three. The main reason for this is that, in order to be usable for interaction, drawing creation and digitising, a particular real device has to perform the role of six notional or 'logical' devices depending on which task it is currently dealing with. These logical devices are:

1 A **locator**: for informing the processor of a particular position on the work surface.
2 A **pick**: for identifying a displayed object.
3 A **choice** or **button**: for choosing from a set of options such as a menu list.

4 A **valuator**: for giving the processor a value such as length or angle.

5 A **string** or **keyboard**: for giving the processor a string of characters for titles and other annotation.

6 A **stroke**: for giving the processor a sequence of locations indicating a continually changing position such as when writing or drawing.

It is possible to use the conventional keyboard to simulate the action of some of these logical devices simply by typing-in locations, values, instructions and so on. Typical of these might be:

DRAW FROM (10,12) TO (100,100)
MOVE BOX-1 TO (30,60)
ROTATE OBJECT-6 BY 45 DEGREES
COLOUR = RED
X = 20

However, whilst this approach has merit for some work, it should be readily apparent that the method is limited in scope and that more appropriate techniques are called for.

For their proper use, many of the devices require the processor continually to display on the screen a graphics cursor usually in the form of a tracking cross which indicates the system's current assessment of location. Moving the pointing element of the input device correspondingly moves the tracking cross. The user can usually fix the position of a particular location by pressing a button or initiating some similar action.

Light pens

A light pen (Figure 3.1) is a device about the size of a chubby ball-point pen which is connected to the processor via a thin cable. When the end of the pen is lightly touched against the output screen and an integral button pressed, the processor is able to detect the fact and, hence, ascertain the location of the position pointed to. Given suitable software, the light pen is particularly useful as a locator as well as a pick and choice device for selecting items already displayed on the screen. In this sense, it provides a very direct medium which many people find attractive. However, the light pen is not suitable for all types of screen and has limited accuracy unless special software techniques are employed to make it act as an

Figure 3.1   Light pen

accurate valuator. Because it works by sensing light from the screen, the light pen cannot always distinguish between two points which are close together and sometimes thinks that screen reflections are legitimate points. Although a certain amount of drawing creation is possible with the light pen, its main use is in interaction.

The mouse

The mouse (Figure 3.2) is a box-shaped electromechanical device small enough to sit comfortably under the hand. It is often mounted on two wheels which are at right angles to its two main axes and is connected to the computer via a cable. This form of mouse is one of the many types of input device which use the setting of a variable resistor to compute location. For the computer to understand the signals resulting from the use of these devices, A-to-D convertors are required which change the analogue signals produced to the digital form the processor needs. The wheels of this type of mouse are fixed to the shafts of two potentiometers which give resistances proportional to the amount of wheel movement. Other forms use a single ball rather than wheels. With these, the amount of movement is recognised by opto-electronic sensors.

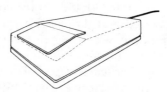

Figure 3.2   Mouse

The mouse has the advantage that it can be used on any flat surface – such as a desk – from where, as it is manoeuvred about, signals are sent to the computer indicating the current values of resistance. This information is then used to calculate the location of the device relative to a previously set origin and is indicated on the screen by means of a tracking cross.

Because there is a certain amount of slippage of the wheels on some surfaces (and because, simply by lifting it up, it is possible to move the device without moving its wheels), the mouse is not a particularly accurate input medium and might be difficult for use in detailed drawing creation (although, with practice, it is possible to become quite proficient at using it for sketching). Experiments have shown that it is especially good as a choice and pick device for pointing to displayed elements and for moving them about the screen in an editing fashion. The mouse has a large number of enthusiastic supporters and is gradually becoming the preferred graphical interaction device for many new systems.

Joysticks, trackballs and thumbwheels

Joysticks, trackballs and thumbwheels are a group of related devices all of which work, like the mouse, by setting variable resistors to values which indicate location in the form of coordinates in the X- and Y-directions. The current location to which the device is notionally pointing is displayed on the screen by the position of a tracking cross or other graphics cursor.

The **joystick** (Figure 3.3) – a name derived from its resemblance to the control column of early aeroplanes – is a short lever pivoted on a ball and socket joint to allow free movement in any direction in the horizontal plane. It is set so that side-to-side movement produces changes in the X-coordinates and front-to-back movement produces changes in the Y-coordinates. Combinations of X- and Y-coordinates arise from diagonal movements. Some joysticks are constructed so that springs return the stick to its central position after movement. Others are designed so that the response of the system to movement is nonlinear in that the further the stick is moved from its central position, the faster the tracking cross travels. A simple joystick is a fairly inexpensive accessory available to most machines and is probably best used as a locator.

The **trackball** (Figure 3.4) is also of ball and socket construction

Figure 3.3 Joystick

with the ball moving freely in its mount. As the ball has to be manipulated with the fingers or palm of the hand, it is made quite large – from 4 to 6 inches (100 to 150 mm) across. The trackball makes a very flexible pointer but its construction is relatively expensive allowing it to be available to comparatively few systems.

As both these devices are highly manoeuvrable, they can be used for direct drawing although they are probably best at tracking, following and pointing at moving elements displayed on the screen rather than any other function. Their manoeuvrability makes them the favourite input devices for many arcade video games although they have serious uses too, notably for pointing to objects on radar output screens where graphic interaction needs to be rapid. Large movements, however, are not easily made with the trackball.

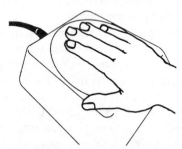

Figure 3.4 Trackball

Thumbwheels (Figure 3.5) are two small knurled-edge wheels set at right angles to one another and embedded in the keyboard of some machines. Close enough together to be manipulated simultaneously by one hand if required, thumbwheels have the advantage

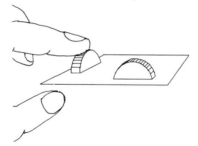

Figure 3.5 Thumbwheels

that the X- and Y-components of a position can be set independently. If, as in a number of Tektronix graphics devices, these components are represented on the screen by separate horizontal and vertical lines rather than a tracking cross, it becomes fairly easy to input accurate figures built-up of lines at right-angles to one another and parallel to the edges of the screen. Such a task is not easily performed by either the joystick or the trackball.

Touchpanels and touchpads

A **touchpanel** (Figure 3.6) is an even more direct device than a light pen in that it is used by simply touching the output screen with the tip of the finger. Such interaction cannot by its very nature allow great accuracy (typical resolutions are up to 50×50 points) so that the device is most useful for choosing items from screen menus or similar tasks but its simplicity and directness of use makes it particularly valuable for casual, untrained persons. Normally, special screens, or perhaps screen covers, are used for touchpanels and

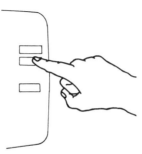

Figure 3.6 Touchpanel

these employ electromagnetic, photoelectric or acoustic ranging techniques.

   Touchpads are a variation of touchpanels and consist of a rectangle of rubber or plastic fixed over a pressure-sensitive platen. Here, too, simple touching and movement of the finger about the platen is sufficient to send appropriate signals to the processor which reflects the results in its positioning of a tracking cross. These devices are not available for all graphic systems and are really only suitable for interaction.

Knobs, dials and sliders

Though rare as graphic input devices, knobs, dials and sliders are used in some systems – perhaps most frequently to set angles of rotation for perspective views of 3-D objects. Like joysticks and trackballs, these devices, too, control variable resistors which require A-to-D convertors for their working.

   So familiar are we with the analogue task of turning knobs and setting sliders to indicate values, that many light pen users create software versions of these devices on their screens. In these, the acts of moving the light pen around a circle or dragging it across a rectangle have the same effects as manipulating hardware knobs and sliders. By use of scaling effects, considerable accuracy can be achieved by such software valuators which can be driven by most of the devices described.

   Another form of device for adjusting potentiometers is the *paddle*, pairs of which are supplied with some personal machines. The paddle is essentially a variable resistor set in a plastic housing and connected to the processor by means of a thin cable. Though not as convenient as thumbwheels, pairs of paddles can perform similar tasks. They are not, however, particularly accurate devices.

Keys and function buttons

Some graphics machines are equipped with sets of keys or buttons which are reserved for special purposes. One such set is often used to control the movement about the screen of a tracking cross. By pressing the appropriate keys, which are sometimes grouped together in the form of a mnemonic pattern (Figure 3.7) of a size

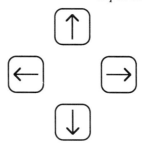

Figure 3.7 Function keys

small enough to fall under the fingers of one hand, users can make the tracking cross take unit steps in the directions needed. Although not a particularly convenient input method, such keys do allow simple drawings to be built up and, as with thumbwheels, the independence of movement provided by each button facilitates the creation of drawings which lie square with the screen edges.

In some cases machines also have sets of special buttons set aside for other graphics tasks – either predefined by the system makers or as designated by the users' own programs. In this latter case, users are often provided with plastic overlays which can fit over the keys to indicate their current functions. Essentially the choice of a button here represents a choice of menu item.

Even if the manufacturers of a system have not included these facilities in their machines, users can fairly easily create software to allow the keys of their conventional keyboard to be used to perform similar tasks although this is not as convenient as having purpose-made provisions.

Tablets and digitisers

A tablet or digitiser consists essentially of three interconnected parts:

1 A thin flat plate (known as the platen or, confusingly, the tablet) which forms the work surface.
2 A pointing device which can be moved about the platen.
3 A controller which converts the electrical signals arising from the interaction of the pointer and the platen into location information relative to some origin. The interaction comes

about generally through electromagnetic induction, occasionally through differences in electrical resistance or, more rarely, by means of acoustic range-finding techniques.

Platens come in a number of sizes, varying from 11 inches (about 280 mm) square to as much as 60 inches (about 1525 mm) square, the larger sizes sometimes having their own adjustable stands. In some versions, the platen is transparent allowing it to be lit from behind for the easier digitising of X-ray plates and other transparencies.

The most usual pointing devices are either a *stylus* (Figure 3.8), a pen-like object which activates a switch when its tip is pressed on the platen; or a *puck* (Figure 3.9). The puck consists of a glass sight on which is scribed a cross-hair target set in a holder housing a number of function buttons which have to be pressed to initiate some action. In most cases both these devices are available as options and it is a matter of preference which one is chosen. The puck is probably better for digitising drawings whilst the stylus is better for pointing, picking and choosing.

The controller acts as a buffer between the pointing device and platen on the one hand, and the processor on the other, and ensures that these elements interact correctly. In some versions, the controller has considerable storage capacity of its own. This allows the location information in the form of coordinates to be stored prior to being sent to the processing unit. Usually the controller allows the selection of either of two modes of digitising: stream mode or point mode.

In stream mode, a continuous stream of points is sent to the

Figure 3.8   Stylus

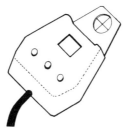

Figure 3.9 Puck

processor at a rate of many per second. This rate is adjustable to allow the points to be either finely or coarsely spaced as the pointer is moved across the platen. This mode is better for inputting curves and irregular lines although, at the higher rates of input, storage capacity is very quickly used up. Stream mode also allows software to detect any movement in the pointing device simply by comparing the coordinates at any moment with those previously received. In this mode the digitiser can act as stroke device. When the system is set for point mode, coordinates are sent only when an appropriate function button or the stylus tip is pressed. This mode is better for choosing menu items and for picking such things as the end points of lines.

Some controllers are also equipped with LED indicators which display the current X- and Y-coordinates of the pointing device; others are sufficiently intelligent to correct for the misalignment of drawings which have been mounted on the skew to the platen edges, rotating the resulting axes to make them square with the platen – a necessary task which must otherwise be performed by the user's own software.

Considerable accuracy of input is achievable by the careful use of tablets and digitisers. Some professional models can resolve to 0.001 inches (0.025 mm) or better, whilst quite inexpensive tablets sold for personal computers can resolve to 0.015 inches (0.38 mm). This accuracy makes the digitiser a common input device for such applications as computer-aided map-making, engineering and architectural design.

It should be noted that what we have described are 2-D digitisers which are particularly useful for transforming existing 2-D drawings into coordinate sets for subsequent manipulation and display. We also require drawings of existing 3-D objects and these are rather more difficult to digitise, especially if they are made up of curved surfaces. Some 3-D digitisers are available but they are rare and should be regarded at this stage in their development as experimental.

Scanners and line followers

Under this heading we have a group of automatic and semi-automatic digitisers whose role is to convert existing drawings or photographs into a form which can be used by the computer. **Scanners** are of two forms: TV camera types (sometimes known as 'frame grabbers') and incremental scanners. The former are used simply by pointing a TV camera at the drawing or other object to be input. The computer hardware and software then convert the picture signals into digital form and the whole is written into storage as a pattern of pixels for later manipulation and treatment. Usually TV devices work only in monochrome with a set number of grey levels. They are relatively cheap and can be obtained as an accessory to some personal systems. The development of solid-state optical sensors, such as charge-coupled-device arrays and optical random access memories which give direct digital video signals, promises to make TV-type scanners even more widely available in the future.

Incremental scanners are electromechanical devices in which a photosensitive head traverses a drawing or photograph in raster fashion converting the light levels it sees into a digital pattern. These devices are expensive and tend to be used only for scientific study and for input of high quality pictures for magazine design. They are of limited availability but make the input of coloured photographic material simple and speedy.

Of course, graphical information given to the computer by either of these types of device is photographic in nature, and subsequent manipulation of the picture is restricted to the same sort of treatment as can be carried out with a photograph – enlargement, left-right reversal, bending, twisting, negative reversal and so on. With the present level of software sophistication, it is not possible to instruct the computer to understand the structure of the image that it is given. Thus, if we scan-in an architect's plan by either of the means described, we cannot ask the system to do such things as highlight all external walls, or delete all internal doors, and so on, because the system does not have enough knowledge about the drawing to do this.

Line followers, on the other hand, do allow the graphic information to be more structured even though it is input semi-automatically. These devices consist of a flat bed over which can travel a scanning head mounted on a gantry-like arm. To use, the scanning head is set manually over one of the lines to be input and started in motion. The device then automatically follows the line, bending and twisting with it and sending details to the processor until it comes to a point where lines cross or fork (or returns to where it started), when it waits to be told which line it should follow next. By setting the scanner to trace lines in a logical order, the processor can be given information on the structure of the drawing. Thus, to return to our example of the architect's plan, if first of all we tell the system that it is tracing external walls, then internal walls, then doors, then furniture and so on, we can ensure that these elements are stored in a way which makes them easily identified for future working. Line followers, however, are expensive and of limited availability.

Input devices generally

In addition to the conventional alphanumeric keyboard, a good graphics system should have at least one other of the input devices we have described, and most manufacturers provide their machines with the facility to attach these as accessories. Although it would be foolish to be too dogmatic on the point, it might be said that serious graphic work cannot be carried out without the assistance of a digitiser or tablet of some sort, and that users with limited resources would be wise to consider the purchase of one of the cheaper sort of these in preference to any of the other devices described.

We must stress that input is a major task in computer graphics: in many practical applications such as computer-aided design of buildings and products as well as computer animation, the inputting of graphical data in a structured form is the most time-consuming and difficult of all the operations. Without adequate hardware and software tools, the task becomes impossibly tedious and error-prone.

4

Output Tasks and Devices

The purpose of a graphic system is twofold. Firstly (and obviously), to produce drawings which are objects in their own right: these include such things as maps; technical drawings; pictorial representations of greater or lesser realism; charts and diagrams for business and scientific purposes; and even animated films. We can call this function the *drawing task*. Secondly (and to those just starting to use computer graphics, not so obviously), to create drawings to assist in further interaction with the system: these include such things as graphical menus; grids and symbols to help in composing drawings or generating commands; software valuators; icons; and tracking crosses. We will refer to this as the *interactive task*.

Unfortunately, the broad span of uses that these two tasks generate are rarely compatible with the capabilities of any single output device (or indeed, of any one technology). For example, technical drawings normally need to be produced on paper or plastic to large size and with a high degree of accuracy in various line styles (though possibly in only one colour) whereas slides or animated movies often need to be created on film stock to 35 mm, or smaller format, and in full colour – sometimes even with realistic shadowing and shading. In neither case do we normally expect such things to be produced in real-time while we are waiting, although it would be nice if they could be. During interaction on the other hand, when we are building-up a technical drawing on the screen, creating, erasing or modifying parts as we go, or when we are previewing the movements of an animation, we expect response to be virtually instantaneous. In addition we want the work be produced on a device which gives us an adequate representation of the appearance of the final result.

Graphic devices generally

Such differences in expectations – as well as the limitations of current technology – have given rise to a variety of output devices to serve our needs. We can consider these to be divided into two broad classes:

1 **Graphic displays** for the real-time interactive task. These include:
   – cathode ray tube devices
   – direct view storage tube (DVST) displays
   – vector refresh displays
   – raster video displays
   – plasma panel displays.
2 **Graphic hardcopy devices** for the drawing task. These devices include:
   – screen copiers
   – electrographic plotters
   – graphic printers
   – vector plotters
   – microfilm recorders.

Despite considerable differences in construction, drawing method and drawing appearance, all these output devices share a common characteristic. This is that they are able to output only to a limited number of points on their drawing surfaces. We can think of the drawing surface effectively as a sheet of gridded paper on which the output device can draw – but with restrictions. Some devices (particularly, plotters, refresh devices and storage tubes) make the restriction only to the endpoints of the lines. Other devices make the restriction to every point on the line. In the first case, a straight line must start and finish within squares of the grid. In the second case, every point along the line must lie within a square of the grid. This means that any sloping lines exhibit a 'staircase' effect and that only vertical or horizontal lines appear to be continuous (Figure 4.1).

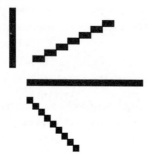

Figure 4.1   Lines made up of pixels

Devices differ by the coarseness or fineness of the grid to which they can draw: a characteristic known as *resolution*. Some personal computers have a resolution of only 40 × 40 squares; the majority of the others run to about 250 × 190, but it is unusual to find home computers with a resolution of more than 600 × 400, even though they might be described as 'high resolution' devices. Professional systems have resolutions varying from 512 × 512 to 1280 × 1024 for raster devices and 4096 × 3120 for DVST systems. Many pen plotters have a resolution of about 46 000 × 25 000 whilst some laser plotters have a resolution of about 11 million × 8 million points! Compare these resolutions with the domestic TV (approximately 800 × 500) and a 35 mm colour slide (about 8000 × 5000).

It is convenient to classify three levels of resolution:

Coarse: up to 256 × 256 points.
Medium: 256 × 256 up to 512 × 512 points.
Fine: 1024 × 1024 points and upwards.

Generally, plasma panels and some video displays have coarse resolution; most video displays have medium resolution; plotters, microfilm recorders, refresh vector displays, DVSTs, as well as some raster displays, have fine resolution.

Displays

Cathode ray tube devices
Vector refresh, raster refresh and DVST displays all employ cathode ray tubes (CRTs). A CRT consists of a vacuum-filled glass

flask with a flattened end which forms the face of the tube (Figure 4.2). A film of phosphor is deposited on the inside surface of this face which gives it the characteristic that any point on which a stream of electrons impinges will emit light. In addition to white, phosphors are available which give out blue, green, yellow, orange or red light and several different phosphors are used when multicolour tubes are needed. At the end of the tube, at right-angles to the flattened face, is the *gun*. This is an electrical component designed to produce a fine beam of electrons controlled to ensure that the correct points on the surface are made to glow. Light from the phosphor does not extinguish immediately the beam ceases to impinge on it but persists for anything from a millionth to a tenth of a second depending on the type used. This is not long enough for an image to register but, fortunately, the electron beam has almost no mass or inertia so it can be switched on or off and moved about the screen at very high speeds allowing any of the surface points to be illuminated many times a second. Thus, frequency of illumination and length of glow can be combined together with our own persistence of vision to help produce a flicker-free image which decays rapidly as soon as the beam is stopped. An image produced by repeated illumination in this way is said to be *refreshed*.

The movement of the beam is produced by elements which electromagnetically deflect the emitted stream of electrons in a controlled way. It is the manner in which the beam is moved which is of primary significance to the creation of the refreshed image. Two

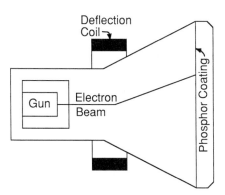

Figure 4.2 Cathode ray tube (CRT)

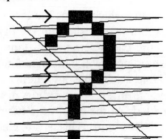

Figure 4.3   Non-interlaced raster

modes of movement are in general use, giving rise to two different lines of product.

In the first, or *raster* mode, the beam follows a fixed pattern of movement which sweeps from side to side and down the screen in a regular arrangement of lines which is repeated from 50 to 60 times a second. The beam is switched on or off depending on whether or not a particular point needs to be refreshed (Figure 4.3). This is the familiar mode in which a TV set works although, in that case, the beam is rarely switched completely off but is simply varied in brightness (or *modulated* as it is known) in order to suit the brightness levels of the scene being depicted. The resulting raster lines are often visible on black and white domestic TV screens. To help minimise this visibility (and to put rather less demand on the communication channels), TV pictures are composed of alternate fields: one consisting of the odd-numbered raster lines and the other consisting of the even-numbered ones. These two fields mesh together to form a complete picture from 25 to 30 times a second

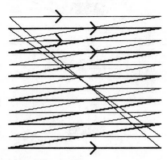

Figure 4.4   Interlaced raster

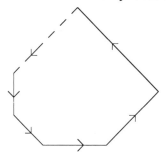

Figure 4.5   A line in vector refresh made

(Figure 4.4). Normally only graphic systems connected to TV receivers use this technique, which is called *interlacing*; most other systems produce single fields containing the whole picture.

In the second mode of refreshing, the beam moves directly to the points required and is switched off during movement and on when the points are reached (Figure 4.5). The resulting pattern is traversed at a refresh rate of 50 to 60 times a second, the order in which the points are visited being determined by the requirements of the particular case. This mode resembles the working of an oscilloscope and is referred to as *vector* or, more frequently (and somewhat confusingly), as *random* mode. The term 'random' is borrowed from probability theory and arises because designers of these systems take the view that one point on the screen is just as likely to need to be illuminated as any other.

In order to produce a picture by either of these means, some part of the computer system has to be continually employed in the refreshing process. In raster devices the normal TV mechanisms do this task, but in vector refresh systems the role has to be played either by the processor itself or, more often, by special-purpose circuitry forming a component called the *display controller*. In both cases, the elements which go to make up the picture have to be stored in hardware designated for refresh storage. Thus, in the simplest refresh system, we have a configuration similar to Figure 4.6 with refresh storage, a display controller and a CRT.

The first CRT systems in use for computer graphics were based on vector refresh mode and these were expensive not only because of the sizes of tubes they employed but also because of their costly

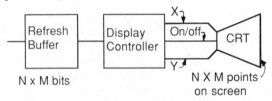

Figure 4.6   Simple mono video refresh system

display controller circuitry. In the late 1960s, however, the US
company Tektronix Inc, which had hitherto specialised in the
manufacture of test oscilloscopes, brought out a new CRT which
revolutionised the situation. Called the *direct view storage tube*
(DVST), the device is able to dispense with the need for continual
refresh by using the tube itself as the store. It does this in a way that,
once drawn, the picture remains on the screen without further
action of either a processor or display controller. This is achieved by
having the electron beam write not directly onto the inside surface
of the tube but onto a fine grid of specially treated wires mounted
just behind the surface. A pattern of electrical charges representing
the drawing being created is formed on the grid by the beam

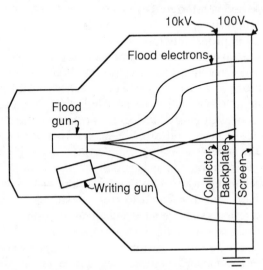

Figure 4.7   Direct view storage tube

impinging on it. This pattern is transferred to the phosphor by means of another gun which continually directs a flood of electrons over the whole area (Figure 4.7). During the first part of the 1970s, the introduction of the DVST was responsible for bringing down the cost of computer graphics to a remarkable degree – in some cases by a factor of ten – and was the basis of most medium- to low-cost displays until the widespread use of raster techniques eight or so years later.

We can now look at the three major types of display in more detail.

Direct view storage tube displays
Apart from their independence from the need for refresh storage, DVSTs are characterised by their high resolution, allowing users to address from 1024×780 to 4096×3120 separate points on the screen depending on type and size. Unfortunately, DVSTs cannot provide full-colour output and do not readily permit lines to be drawn at different brightness levels. These limitations prevent their use for shading in various levels of grey or in different colours. Because of this, DVST devices are best used for drawings formed out of lines (or *vectors* as they are frequently called) and this makes them the favoured medium for technical and scientific rather than for pictorial purposes.

Although storage tubes are extremely useful for line drawings, their main disadvantage is that their screens cannot be erased on a selective basis: whenever any part of a drawing needs to be revised, the whole screen must be cleared and the corrected version re-drawn. This redrawing process can take tens of seconds if the drawing is very complicated. For this reason, ordinary storage tubes are not the best devices for dynamic interaction. Recognising this, some new Tektronix devices combine their valuable DVST characteristics with a limited capacity for refresh working and this allows up to 1000 short vectors to be drawn in refresh mode. Such an added facility, of course, increases the cost of the device. Light pens cannot be used with DVSTs although other methods of screen interaction are available.

Vector refresh displays
Whilst often more expensive than DVST systems, those based on

random refresh technology have a number of advantages. They can be used for high-quality drawings in lines of various thicknesses and colours; shaded areas can be displayed; above all, they allow the dynamic creation, partial erasure and recreation of pictures. When combined with very fast display processing, this facility permits graphics objects to be moved about the screen, changed in size or re-orientated in real-time thus presenting the immediacy of smoothly animated pictures. Because the whole picture needs to be continually redrawn at 50 to 60 times a second, any part of it can be selectively erased or changed during the redrawing process. This can be done either by program or in response to user's requests via a light pen or similar device. Like storage tubes, vector refresh devices are capable of very high resolution. Unlike DVSTs, though, they suffer from the drawback that, as the number of vectors on the screen approaches an upper limit, the display processor and beam have more and more work to do and find it harder to keep up with the refresh rate. When this happens, a disturbing flicker of the image can be seen. Just a few years ago, flicker arose when the number of vectors displayed was relatively small and this defect tended to give random refresh devices a bad name. Some medium-cost machines now exist which can show over 40 000 lines without flicker. It might be thought that such a number of lines is large enough to cater for any conceivable drawing. Bear in mind though that circles and other curves have to be made up of numerous vectors short enough to make the curve appear smooth. Circles made of 150 or even 250 lines are commonplace and, at these numbers, only around 150–200 circles can be drawn before flicker begins to appear.

Raster video displays
Most of the most recent and rapid developments in graphics hardware and software have been concerned with raster video displays. In these, the electron beam traverses the screen in a fixed pattern, visiting each point in turn and illuminating those which represent the drawing to be shown. Raster systems can be made at low cost, particularly when standard TV screens or video monitors are used. They are reliable; coloured lines or areas can be easily produced; animation is possible; and, unlike with vector refresh hardware, there is no flicker however much information is shown on the screen.

Unfortunately, these attractive advantages are offset by the comparatively coarse resolution that the cheaper raster devices can offer. This defect comes about because devices based on the standard European TV screen use a raster of only 625 lines (525 lines are standard in the USA). Furthermore, for technical reasons, not all the lines are displayable, with the result that only about 90 per cent of them can actually be used. Computer displays using TV screens based on the US standards, therefore, can only display about 480×600 points and those based on the European standards, 575×760. For computer work and experimental TV, 1000 line tubes are available giving resolutions of over 1000 horizontally by 1000 vertically, but these are expensive. Cheaper raster displays have resolutions of 256×256 or 512×512 points.

It might be thought that having a resolution which is about one-eighth of that obtainable by the other systems would make raster devices especially unappealing but this is not so. For many applications, particularly those where full colour or shading is needed, we find that the advantages far outweigh the disadvantages. However, as a consequence of the coarse spacing of points, raster drawings suffer from the annoying 'staircase' effect mentioned earlier. This defect can only be overcome by the use of software or hardware techniques known as *anti-aliasing*.

The points displayed on raster screens are pixels consisting of small squares or rectangles and it is sometimes arranged that there is a digital cell in the computer corresponding to each pixel – an arrangement known as *bit-mapping*. As each cell can contain a zero (for no illumination) or a one (for illumination), a 512×512 cell store of 32K bytes will only cope with drawings in one colour on a 512×512 screen. A larger store is needed if multicoloured pictures are to be produced and some full-colour systems have as many as $512 \times 512 \times 24$ storage cells, making a store of three-quarters of a million bytes for pictures alone. The array of storage cells are formed by integrated circuit chips made up into a device known as a *frame buffer*. The job of the frame buffer is to accept the digital picture from the processor and present it to the screen via the display controller.

SEEING COLOUR

The eye is sensitive to wavelengths of light between about 380 and 780 nanometres (a nanometre has the abbreviation nm and is one thousand millionth of a metre). Wavelengths at the shorter end of the range are perceived as violet and at the longer end as red. In normal lighting conditions we are most sensitive to light of 555 nm wavelength which we see as yellowish green.

To achieve its reaction to light, the eye acts something like a small spherical camera; it has a lens and iris system at one side and a light-sensitive coating opposite. This coating is called the retina and consists of two types of light-sensitive cells: *rods*, which deal with low light conditions, and *cones*, which deal with normal light and colour. The cells are connected to the optic nerve which channels the signals they produce to the brain for interpretation. There are about 130 million rods and cones but they are not distributed equally over the whole retina and rods outnumber cones by about 17 to 1. The majority of cones are concentrated in one tiny spot called the *fovea* where there are no rods at all. In order for us to see anything clearly, we must direct its image onto the fovea, a process which we do unconsciously by constant small movements of the eye.

There are three types of cone: red-sensitive, green-sensitive and blue-sensitive. When light of appropriate wavelengths falls on these they combine to send signals to the brain which are interpreted into the correct sensations of colour. Thus all colours we can see are combinations of red, green and blue light.

COLOUR IN TV AND RASTER DISPLAYS

Just as the eye achieves its reception of colour by the interaction of cells sensitive to red, green or blue light, so colour TV creates colour by the selective illumination of red, green and blue phosphors. The phosphors are often arranged on the screen as minute dots set in a triangular pattern, as in Figure 4.8. As the dots are so small and so

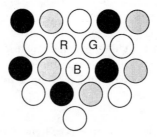

Figure 4.8   Triangular pattern of phosphor dots

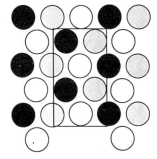

Figure 4.9 Group of phosphors making a pixel (as in this case, grouping does not always allow square pixels)

close together, the eye cannot see them as individual spots of light at normal viewing distances. Thus when adjacent dots of different colours are illuminated, we see them merged into one colour. A pixel can consist of just one triad of phosphors or a group of them as shown in Figure 4.9. Course resolution devices have large groups of triads.

Three electron guns, one for the red phosphors, one for the green and one for the blue, are accurately focused onto the dots and can make them glow in varying intensities. For TV, the intensities are continuously variable by analogue circuitry but, for computer displays, the control is digital and hence goes in steps. In the simplest colour graphics systems, the steps are coarse – perhaps being restricted just to on and off.

Table 4.1

Colour	Red gun	Green gun	Blue gun
Black	off	off	off
Blue	off	off	on
Green	off	on	off
Cyan	off	on	on
Red	on	off	off
Magenta	on	off	on
Yellow	on	on	off
White	on	on	on

Three guns have eight possible combinations of on and off so, if we include black and white as colours, only eight are possible with such a coarse setting. The colours achievable are shown in Table 4.1.

In order to store and manipulate the colours, we must arrange for part of the computer to hold a representation of the pixels. As we pointed out earlier, a 512×512 pixel screen would need 512×512 bits (32K bytes) of storage to hold a monochrome picture. For monochrome pictures we need one bit per pixel, for eight-colour pictures we need three bits per pixel. These bits are often arranged in what are known as bit-planes, one for each colour gun (Figure 4.10) and the setting of the bits in the planes determines the colours to be displayed. Thus, if a bit is set to 1 for gun-on and to 0 for gun-off, Table 4.1 will look like Table 4.2.

Table 4.2

Colour	Bit-plane 1	Bit-plane 2	Bit-plane 3
Black	0	0	0
Blue	0	0	1
Green	0	1	0
Cyan	0	1	1
Red	1	0	0
Magenta	1	0	1
Yellow	1	1	0
White	1	1	1

For more than eight colours, more bit-planes are needed. If two bit-planes are assigned to each gun and control their intensities by means of digital-to-analogue converters (DACs) as in Figure 4.11, we can arrange for 32 colours to be displayed. This is achievable because each bit-plane can have both bits off, one or other of them on, or both on. For even more colours, further bit-planes are necessary although it is rare for more than 24 planes to be used in all. A 24-bit-plane configuration is expensive in storage but would actually cater for 16 777 216 different colours. Even if every pixel of a 1024×1024 screen were set to a different colour, it would be impossible for us to display over 16 million colours at once so, for practical purposes, we can make do with a much smaller subset of

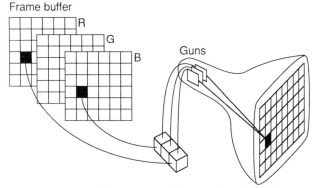

Figure 4.10 Eight colour system with three bit-planes

this pallete on any one drawing. A technique to minimise storage and yet still give us a very wide range of colours is colour table mapping.

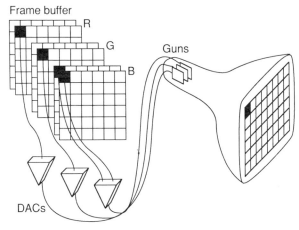

Figure 4.11 Sixty-four colour system with six bit-planes

COLOUR TABLE MAPPING

As we have seen, the setting of bits in three planes will only produce eight different combinations and, if these are used to control the colour guns directly, we can only have the colours black, blue, green, cyan, red, magenta, yellow and white. However, if we had an

eight-entry table of 24 bits width and used these bits to control the
guns, our bit-planes could point to entries in the table and thus
choose any eight of the 16 million colours available (Figure 4.12).
Our bit-planes would be in one to one correspondence with the
screen pixels but would indicate for each a number in the range 0–7.

Many professional computer graphics systems have 12 bit-planes
and a table of 24 bits width. These allow us to choose (for any
particular picture) 4096 colours out of the full pallette of 16 million.
With such a configuration a 512 × 512 pixel screen needs 384 K bytes
of picture storage and 12 K bytes of table. Some personal systems

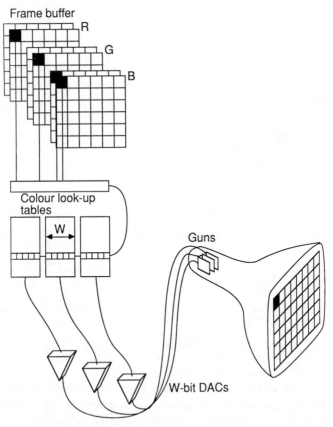

Figure 4.12   Colour setting by means of look-up tables

have smaller pallettes and colour tables. A popular configuration is 256 colours out of a pallette of 4096. This means that the colour table is 12 bits wide and that there are eight bit-planes available. In this case, a 512×512 pixel screen needs 256K bytes of picture storage and 384 bytes of table.

The formulae for determining the number of colours and bit-planes is:

Number of colours in pallette $= 2^W$
Number of displayable colours $= 2^N$
where W = Bit width of table, and
     N = Number of bit-planes

Colour tables not only reduce the amount of storage necessary but can also be used to produce a limited form of animation. This is achieved by dynamically assigning colours to the table so that some elements of the drawing are changed from the background colour into foreground colours in a way that makes them appear to move from one part of the screen to another.

Plasma panel displays
Plasma panel displays are built on entirely different principles to CRTs. Rather than exploiting the luminescent properties of phosphors, these displays rely on the fact that an inert gas (such as neon) glows in the presence of an electric field. Two categories of plasma devices exist:

1 Direct current (DC) devices, normally used for smallish, character-only displays.
2 Alternating current (AC) devices, normally used for both text and graphics.

AC panels consist of a thin layer of neon gas sandwiched between two plates of glass; one incorporating a horizontal pattern of electrodes and the other incorporating a vertical pattern (Figure 4.13). By passing an alternating current through the appropriate X and Y electrodes, the gas around their intersection is made to glow. By means of this, individual pixels can be illuminated and will remain so without any refresh mechanism until some positive electronic action is taken to extinguish them.

AC plasma panels with their thin, flat format are now made in

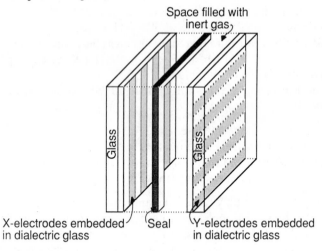

Space filled with
inert gas

Glass

Glass

X-electrodes embedded
in dialectric glass

Seal

Y-electrodes embedded
in dialectric glass

Figure 4.13 Plasma AC panel with transparent X–Y electrodes

sizes and resolutions that make them practical alternatives to
graphic CRTs. Flicker-free devices having 768×960 monochrome
pixels, each only one third of a millimetre across, are now possible
but, as yet, their use in graphics is not widespread. Both plasma and
other forms of flat screen, non-CRT technology are likely to have
considerable impact on graphic system design in the future and,
over the next few years, will make a real challenge to the present
supremacy of the CRT.

Graphic hardcopy devices

In addition to showing drawings on screens, we also want drawings
on paper. Because of this, the growth in development of different
types of graphic display has been accompanied by a corresponding
growth in the development of hardcopy devices, particularly for
reproducing colour output. Essentially, these devices fall into five
broad types:

1   Screen copiers.
2   Electrographic plotters.
3   Graphic printers.
4   Vector plotters.
5   Microfilm recorders.

Each type has its particular technology, resolution, colour capability and cost range although, being electromechanical devices, they are all usually more expensive than displays of equivalent quality.

Screen copiers

It is difficult to take good colour photographs directly from the screens of raster graphic colour displays. The problem comes about for three reasons:

1 Very often the surface of the display screen is curved and this gives rise to a picture distortion in photographs. We hardly notice this curvature when viewing the display itself but it seems to be exaggerated in photographs.
2 The sensitivity of colour film is balanced either for average daylight or for tungsten light and this results in the incorrect exposure of some screen colours.
3 The inconvenience of setting-up of the camera, particularly as the comparatively long exposure times needed interferes with the normal use of the display.

In the last few years, a group of special cameras, called *screen copiers*, have come onto the market and these quite successfully overcome the problems of photography. The original research and development work in this area was carried out by the Polaroid Corporation and Dunn Instruments Inc. and, for this reason, such devices are sometimes called 'Dunn Cameras' although only those produced by Dunn should actually be given this name.

Various copiers differ in outward appearance, cost and performance, but all are based on the same essential principle: a light-tight box, independent of the screen, containing a small, flat-faced, single-colour CRT in front of which is a red, green and blue filter wheel together with a camera system, all under microprocessor control. In producing a photograph, the same raster video signal which creates the picture on the display is used by the screen copier. This signal is fed to the copier where, first, its red component is displayed on the internal screen and photographed through the red filter; then the green component is photographed through the green filter; and, finally, the blue component is photographed through the blue filter. This process takes up to about a minute depending on the film used. All three components are superimposed on one picture to produce a composite full-colour image. The fact that the exposure for each of the primary colours is made separately means that the individual exposure times can be properly set to match the differential colour sensitivity of the particular film used. (As it turns out, the correct exposure time for red is about three or four times that of the other two colours.) This ability to control exposure differentially and the use of the flat screen gives rise to a high fidelity reproduction in bright, saturated colours. An added advantage is that slight changes in colour rendition are possible without the need to re-generate the image. Some screen copiers can also make colour copies from monochrome displays.

A number of film formats are available for these systems including:

1   8 × 10 inch and 4 × 5 inch Polaroid prints.
2   8 × 10 inch overhead projection transparencies.
3   35 mm transparencies.
4   16 mm and 35 mm cine film (some copiers only).

The larger prints are quite expensive and it is necessary for an operator to be in attendance to deal with the film handling. Screen copiers, though, present the only method of reproducing exactly what is seen on the display. Other forms of screen copier are those which can provide only black-and-white or grey scale reproductions either from the screen image or from storage. Earlier versions of these devices used photosensitive paper which passed in front of an integral CRT to be exposed and then automatically fixed by thermal means. Recent devices, however, tend to use dry-toner electrostatic principles. The photosensitive paper types are fairly expensive in cost per copy but are excellent for making fast working copies of output for tests or checking purposes.

Electrographic plotters

Electrographic plotters produce their images electrostatically on dialectrically coated medium. The image gets onto the medium, usually paper or perhaps plastic, by means of a row or two of tiny styluses as in Figure 4.14. The computer uses these to generate small raster-scanned electrostatic dots at a pitch of 100 or 200 to the inch. The paper then passes through a fine powder, called *toner*, which adheres to the charged points and is fixed in the pattern of the

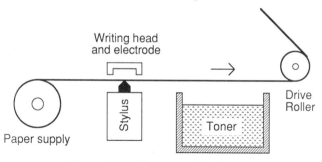

Figure 4.14 Electrographic plotter

image. High-quality black-and-white drawings can be produced by these means on the medium which comes in long rolls and in a variety of widths. Recently, too, colour systems have been developed but these are very expensive.

The devices are extremely fast when plotting but, because the drawing has to be produced line by line from top to bottom, it is necessary to present the image to the plotter in raster-fashion. In considering the total time needed to make a copy, the time for the computer to sort and *rasterise* the image has to be taken into account. This can be quite long if small computers are used. Some plotters have their own processors to take care of rastering. Even without these, the speed advantage of electrostatic plotters is marked (especially if multiple plots of the same picture are needed – where rasterisation is only done once). For example, a chart 45 ins × 36 ins (1143 mm × 914 mm) containing about 15 000 lines can be drawn in about 45 secs. This time includes for sorting and rasterising the image and should be compared with the ten or so minutes taken by a fast pen plotter.

Unfortunately, electrographic plotters are fairly expensive and are not yet having an impact on personal computing.

Graphic printers
Graphic printers make their drawings by use of the dot matrix principle where tiny hammers impact on a ribbon, similar to a conventional printer. Recent versions can produce limited colour output by the use of coloured ribbons and the various devices differ

only by the number of colours available and the way the ribbons are arranged.

In some versions, the ribbon is divided horizontally into four colours: yellow, magenta, cyan and black. The print-head passes along the drawing line by line as many times as is necessary to create the limited range of colours that this machine allows and no colour mixing is attempted. Other types use a four-colour ribbon divided into four-colour sections along its length. The machine interfaces directly with the CRT and prints the complete picture one colour at a time, starting with all the yellow parts, then the magenta, then the cyan and, finally, the black. Overlapping of colours produces red, green and blue. Yet other forms use separate ribbon cassettes for the four colours so that any one can be easily changed if it is more frequently used than the others.

These machines are useful and relatively cheap – particularly as they can double as conventional text printers. However, they cannot yet be considered as true graphics devices if high-colour fidelity is required, although, with a little software effort in creating patterns, their apparent colour range can be extended. At present, graphics printers are probably best used for diagrams and charts rather than pictorial graphics.

Vector plotters

For our purposes, we can assume that vector plotters fall into three classes:

1 Pen plotters.
2 Ink jet plotters.
3 Laser plotters.

Pen plotters are very familiar to us all and were probably the first form of graphics hard copy device to be used (developing from pre-computer X–Y recorders used in laboratories and industry). There are a wide range of types and manufacturers to choose from, but basically there are three forms of machine available:

1 Rotary or drum.
2 Flat bed.
3 'Turtle'.

In rotary plotters, the paper (or other drawing medium) is fed onto a drum which moves it forwards and backwards under a pen which travels from side to side. The combination of these movements, together with the appropriate raising or lowering of the pen, produces the drawing. In flat bed plotters, the paper is fixed in position on a platen and the pen moves from side to side on an arm which travels backwards and forwards along the platen. In 'turtle' plotters, drawing pens are carried by a small turtle-like trolley (Figure 4.15) which (although attached to the computer by a ribbon cable) is free to roam about the paper and which can be laid on any flat surface.

In all cases, the composite directions of movement are normally limited to eight at 45 degrees apart. It is the job of the plotting software to ensure that the correct combination of incremental movements is chosen in order to draw the image properly.

Plotters can be categorised by their:

1 Resolution.
2 Degree of intelligence.
3 Size of plot.
4 Cost.

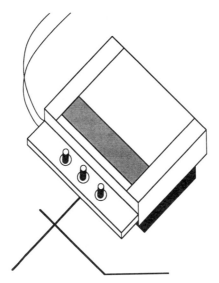

Figure 4.15 Trolley-type plotter

Resolution ranges from 0.001 ins to 0.01 ins (0.025 mm to 0.25 mm) and, whilst the higher resolutions give better drawings, they put an increased burden on the computer and are generally slower to plot. However, with plotters having sufficient intelligence, it is possible to preset the resolution needed (both for the plot and any accompanying text) so that a lower resolution can be used for previewing drawings before a final, full resolution, plot. In addition, many intelligent plotters have built-in functions allowing them to generate such things as circles and arcs with simple commands from the computer. This ability, combined with storage facilities in the plotter, often lets the computer send substantial parts of the drawing to it at speed allowing the computer to be temporarily released to get on with other activities whilst the plotter deals with the information it has. Some plotters can also be driven by separate magnetic tape units allowing them to work off-line. Off-line plotting, of course, obviates the need to tie up the computer for long periods but substantially increases the cost of hardware.

Plotters are available to cope with a wide variety of drawing sizes from 10 ins (250 mm) wide to 72 ins (1829 mm). Both rotary and flat bed plotters allow rolls of paper to be used, thus facilitating drawings of these widths and any reasonable length. Flat bed plotters, on the other hand, also allow the use of preprinted standard sheets – a facility often desired for CAD purposes, but note that US devices rarely use the A-standard paper sizes common in Europe. Drawings can not only be output to paper: Mylar and other types of drafting film as well as cel are possible media.

Multiple-pen devices are also common. These allow the graphics program to choose pen thicknesses or colours to suit particular circumstances. Two, six or even eight pen systems are common. Felt-tip, ball-point or wet-ink drafting pens are all available. Wet ink pens probably give the best plot but are subject to clogging and are slightly troublesome to use. Their range of thicknesses, however, is very good.

Costs of these devices vary according to size and facilities provided but even the smallest rotary or flat bed plotter is likely to cost as much as a personal computer. Turtle plotters, on the other hand, are quite cheap but cannot, as yet, be seen as professional devices. Generally it can be said that, size for size, pen plotters are cheaper than electrographic plotters.

Ink jet plotters use a continuous stream of electrically charged ink which is sprayed at a sheet of paper through a high-voltage field (Figure 4.16). The field is switched on and off by the controlling mechanism according to whether the ink should or should not be deposited. These devices are quiet and speedy but, presently, give colours of limited saturation. Much work is going on into their development and they are likely to be seen more and more as alternatives to screen copiers especially in personal computing. They are relatively inexpensive – the cheapest being about the cost of a good printer. Their major disadvantage is that the jet heads become clogged with ink so that frequent cleaning and similar maintenance is essential.

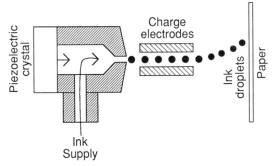

Figure 4.16 Construction of an ink jet plotter

Laser plotters use a low-powered laser to reproduce a line or tone image onto a photosensitive drum. Sensitised areas of the drum acquire coloured toner as in the standard colour xerography process, and this toner is transferred to the paper over which the drum rolls. The process occurs three times, once for each primary reflective colour (cyan, magenta, yellow), and these mix to produce other colours as with some graphic printers.

These plotters are fast and quiet and can double as high-quality text printers. They are, however, rather expensive, although new, single colour devices aimed at the personal computer market are gradually becoming available.

Microfilm recorders

These have the same basic architecture as screen copiers in that they have a camera system set in front of a flat, black-and-

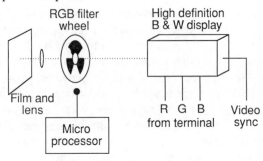

Figure 4.17   Microfilm recorder

white, high-resolution CRT and that filming takes place through a computer-controlled colour filter wheel (Figure 4.17). Unlike screen copiers, however, microfilm recorders create their images directly from computer instructions and are thus independent of their user's own display.

They are extremely expensive, fine resolution devices designed for direct recording of multicoloured images onto film media in various formats. These formats include 35mm movie and still, 16mm movie, microfiche and microfilm, each of which requires its own interchangeable camera system (which, in themselves, are more costly than many small computers).

Made to cope with large volumes of work, they can perform in both vector and raster modes using their own built-in mini- or micro-computers. Their present size and cost makes microfilm recorders comparatively rare devices which are unlikely to be encountered by non-professional graphics programmers.

5

Computer Graphics Programming

The importance of mathematics

Unfortunately for those who have always regarded mathematics as something of a mystery, it is not possible to do effective graphics programming (except in mosaic style) without having at least a working knowledge of geometry, trigonometry and algebra. At the level we require, these subjects are not difficult to understand and a few hours detailed working through the mathematics of the next few chapters and Appendix 1 will be amply repaid when the time comes to write workable programs and to study more advanced texts.

We need mathematics for two reasons. Firstly, in order to describe to the computer the details of the objects we wish to draw – a process known as *geometrical modelling*. Secondly, in order to manipulate the representations of these objects within the machine and to display them as we wish. It is perfectly possible to devise graphic systems which allow us to create drawings directly by means of a tablet and pointing device, thereby dispensing with the need for geometrical modelling altogether. Such systems, often known as paint systems, have a program which translates the movement of a stylus or mouse into lines on the screen. This allows us to depict an object or scene by means of a sketch. To help us in this task, the system gives us aids for drawing straight lines, circles, ellipses and so on as well as assistance for quickly colouring-in or erasing parts of the picture.

Graphics done in this fashion (Figure 5.1) can be very effective but requires considerable artistic flair and ability to produce. In addition, any further manipulation of drawings created by paint systems is restricted to the same sort of treatment that can be applied to photographs. This means that a paint system can enlarge or reduce a drawing, reverse it or change its colours. It cannot, however, alter any of its essential form. If, for example, we had sketched a side view of a house, we could not ask a paint system to give us a view from the front or a perspective view of the whole because the system has no understanding of the 3-D nature of the object our sketch depicts. In other words, the computer has no model of the object we are displaying.

Figure 5.1   A 'painted' image

To enable us to take any views of objects on demand we have to carry out four separate tasks each of which requires the use of mathematics (Figure 5.2). These are:

1 **Modelling** – where we describe the object in sufficient detail to enable the computer to 'understand' its geometry; we also call this *object description.*
2 **Transformation** – where we manipulate the model by movements, rotations and viewing calculations in order to put it in the right form for display.
3 **Clipping** – where we trim the drawing to the dimensions of the display surface to make sure it will fit within the boundaries.
4 **Display** – where we draw the view on some output device.

We will see later that the precise point in the process at which we clip is important and that this depends on the capabilities of our output device. In some cases, we must clip before we send the drawing

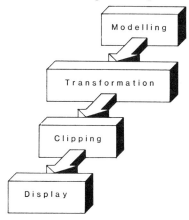

Figure 5.2 The graphic process

information to the display. In other cases, it is possible to send the unclipped information and for the device itself to do the clipping. Although, in terms of the final drawing, the results will be the same, the actual performance will be different. A device which can handle its own clipping is likely to be faster than one not able to do this.

After a review of the principles of coordinates, in our next few chapters we look at the ways in which we can model, transform, clip and display 2-D objects.

6

Modelling: Coordinates

At the heart of almost any method of geometric modelling is the coordinate system. This give us ways of representing positions in 2-D and 3-D space by means of sets of numbers. A point in 2-D space can be uniquely defined by two numbers and in 3-D space by three numbers. To avoid ambiguity, the numbers must be put in a generally agreed order: for example, Figure 6.1 shows that the point represented in a coordinate system by (1,2) is quite different from point (2,1). The coordinate system is a framework for properly locating points and one form of these frameworks is a pair or triple of axes (depending on whether 2- or 3-D representations are required) set orthogonally to one another. By orthogonal, we mean at right angles in a way that the lines forming the corners of a cube are at right angles (Figure 6.2).

There are a variety of other possible coordinate systems that

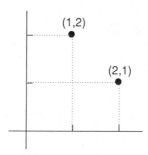

Figure 6.1   Coordinates

Figure 6.2 Orthogonal axes

can be used to describe objects but we will confine ourselves to this, the more usual form known as a *cartesian coordinate system* – a name derived from that of Descartes (1596–1650), the French philosopher/mathematician who did much to establish the principles of coordinate geometry.

2-D coordinates

For a 2-D cartesian coordinate system, just two axes are needed and it is customary for these to be arranged so that the first number in the coordinate pair is represented on a horizontal axis with numbers increasing towards the right, and the second number, on a vertical axis with numbers increasing in the upwards direction, and this is the convention we employ in this book. The point (0,0) where the axes intersect is called the origin. As indicated in Figure 6.3, coordinates can be positive or negative and can be decimal fractions as well as whole numbers.

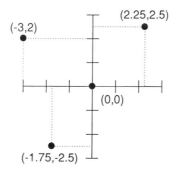

Figure 6.3 Coordinates

3-D coordinates

In 3-D coordinate systems, three axes are needed: the two required for 2-D, plus a third which is set at right angles to both these. Whilst the first two coordinates are normally represented in the same way as in the 2-D case, the third coordinate can be represented in one of two ways. If we think of the 2-D part of the coordinate system as lying in the plane of this page, the third number is represented by the axis going from your eye through the origin on the page. The numbers can either increase as they go away from you, defining a left-handed coordinate system (Figure 6.4a), or they can increase as they come towards you, in which case a right-handed system is defined (Figure 6.4b).

Thus, in a left-handed 3-D system, for instance, the coordinates (2,3,1) represent a point 2 units to the right of the origin, 3 units above the origin, and 1 unit from the origin in the direction away from the eye. The point (0,0,0) represents the origin in both left-handed and right-handed systems.

Although programs using left-handed systems can be converted to right-handed with little difficulty, it is essential that the one to be used is understood from the outset or great confusion can result. In this book, we use the *left-handed* system.

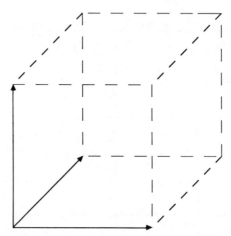

Figure 6.4a   Left-handed coordinate system

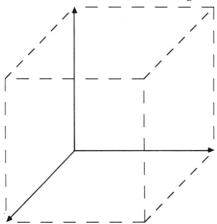

Figure 6.4b   Right-handed coordinate system

Coordinate forms

For computer graphics purposes, two basic forms of coordinates need to be considered:

1   **World coordinates**, which are those we use to define the objects and elements we want to depict; they are the coordinates used to model the real world.
2   **Device coordinates**, which are those used by the device itself to display the representation; they are the coordinates we use to view the model.

Because of the differences of units used, it is rare for these two forms to coincide even in the 2-D case.

World coordinates

In our application programs, we need to express our coordinates in the units we use in real life. Some of us require 2-D systems, others require 3-D. Factory managers, for example, might want a chart showing maintenance costs against time, so would use a 2-D co-ordinate set with pounds sterling or dollars on one axis and years on the other; sales managers might need numbers of items sold set against months; some scientists, on the other hand, might need to work in miles, nanoseconds, Angstrom units, parsecs or what have

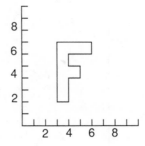

Figure 6.5   Letter F

you; designers might need to prepare drawings of 3-D objects measured in metres and millimetres. Occasionally, as with the letter 'F' of Figure 6.5, we might use special units just devised for the purpose. Positive and negative values of these units must be catered for, and 2-D systems as well as right- or left-handed 3-D systems have to be allowed.

Some people, too, might make use not only of special units but also of other coordinate forms. One such is the polar coordinate system, where the position of a point is defined by means of an angle and a distance (Figure 6.6). This form of coordinates is useful for a number of purposes but we will assume that, by the time computer graphics is needed, such *user coordinates* have been translated by program into cartesian world coordinates.

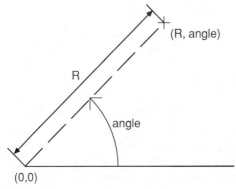

Figure 6.6   Polar coordinate system where position depends on distance, R, and angle

Device coordinates

Device coordinates relate to the dimensions of the 2-D display surface we use. Many displays assume a coordinate system with the origin at the bottom left-hand corner and the positive axes running right and upwards (Figure 6.7). A few raster displays (the Apple II and the Macintosh, for instance) have their origins at the top left-hand corner with the positive axes running to the right and downwards. A rarer few locate their origins in the centre of the screen. Before programming any graphics system, you must be sure you know which of the arrangements has been adopted, or you will not be able to produce the results you envisage.

At present, device coordinates appear to be set in any units which catch the manufacturers' fancies. They may be inches or, perhaps, centimetres, but are more likely to be quite arbitrary units such as, say, 0 to 130, 0 to 100, 0 to 279, or 0 to 1023 and so on. The newly adopted GKS standard for computer graphics requires that the device coordinates be in real dimensions, measured in metres, with the origin at the bottom left, but there has not yet been enough time for this standard to take widespread effect. Part of the job of a computer graphics program is to convert the world coordinates to device coordinates without users having to trouble themselves with the actual details of the process.

In well-structured graphics systems, three related concepts assist in this task: normalised device coordinates, windows and viewports.

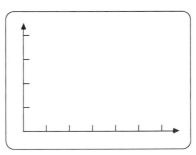

Figure 6.7 Usual form of screen coordinate system (increasing to right and upwards)

Normalised device coordinates (NDCs)

NDCs assume that the dimensions of the display surface run from 0.0 to 1.0 in both directions, regardless of its actual size or shape. The origin for this 2-D coordinate system is set at the bottom left-hand corner of the display surface (Figure 6.8). NDCs are used as the intermediate units between world and device coordinates with the aim of separating the computation of a picture from its display. Thus we can compute the picture as if it were to be displayed on a notional device whose dimensions are 1.0×1.0 and then scale this information to the dimensions of the actual devices to be used. This has the added advantage that, if the normalised information is filed away on a disc or tape, it can later be displayed on any new device with no alteration other than appropriate scaling.

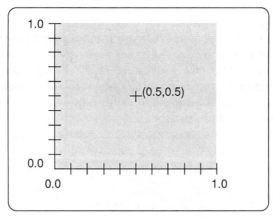

Figure 6.8   Normalised device coordinates (drawing surface shaded-in)

Windows

When we wish to create a drawing, we initially have to decide on how much of the real world it is to depict. Designers of, say, table lamps who want to do working drawings of their products might conclude that the only part of the world they need consider is a cube of 1 metre in each direction. This is because any lamp they need to draw would not be more than 1 m wide nor more than 1 m high. In other words, they have a 'window' which is 1 m wide by 1 m high. In order to exploit the fact that any product is symmetrical about its vertical axes, it is likely that they will want to define their window in the horizontal direction as ranging from -500 mm to $+500$ mm and in the vertical direction from 0 to 1000 mm (Figure 6.9).

Historians, on the other hand, might have real and estimated data on population changes from 85 BC to AD 2085 and, if they wish to plot all of this, will have a window which extends horizontally from -85 to $+2085$, and vertically from, say, $-20\ 000$ to $+1\ 000\ 000$. Alternatively, they might wish to display only that part of the data covering the period from the Discovery of America to the beginning of the First World War – in which case, their window would range from $+1492$ to $+1914$ in the horizontal direction.

From these examples, we can see that windows are a 2-D concept and can be symmetrical or asymmetrical as well as of any proportion and dimension. In addition, they can be bigger or smaller than the dimensions of the things they are to portray. When they are smaller, only the section of the world falling within the window will be displayed. By varying the sizes of the window, we can change the scale and proportion of the view – doubling the window dimensions halves the scale of the view; halving the dimensions doubles the scale. However, when we increase the scale, parts of the view will fall outside the display surface and this can cause difficulties unless

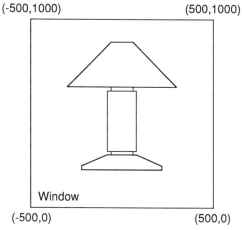

Figure 6.9 Table lamp

the display device is designed to cope or unless our program takes the necessary precautions.

One way of dealing with the problem would be to search through the data and omit anything which is outside the window. This procedure would work for the historians' information – we would simply start processing and displaying at the 1492 date and finish at 1914 – but this solution would not work in most cases. In particular, to draw a perspective view of an object requires that all the data about its geometry be processed even though only part of the projection is displayed. Thus it is necessary to compute the whole drawing and then clip any of the lines which fall outside the window. This is a simple but not a trivial mathematical process – lines running across the corner of the window, for instance, have to be clipped at both ends and, as it is impossible to decide ahead of time which lines must be clipped, all have to be passed through the clipping routine. Some display devices are able to perform the clipping themselves so that the user simply defines a window and sends the whole drawing to the device which then displays only the relevant part.

Viewports

Our discussion on windowing tacitly assumed that the whole display surface would be used to show the windowed drawing. However, it

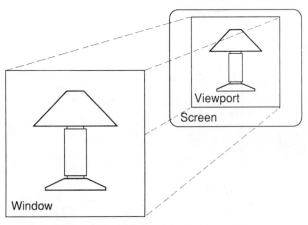

Figure 6.10   Window/viewport mapping

is quite likely that we will wish to use only part of the display – either to leave room for text or to allow multiple drawings to be shown on the same viewing surface. In order to accommodate this require-ment we have the concept of the *viewport*, which is a rectangular portion of the display surface defined in device or normalised device coordinates onto which we map the desired window (Figure 6.10).

Three important points have to be noted about viewports:

1   Unless distortion is to result, the proportions of both windows and viewports must match.
2   Whilst viewports can be defined as smaller than display surfaces, in most systems they must not be defined as larger or unexpected results can occur.
3   Viewports can, if needed, overlap on the display surface.

Exercises

6.1   We saw in Figure 6.1 that the order in which we give coordinate numbers is vital and that the point (X,Y) is generally quite different from the point (Y,X). If we reverse all the coordinate pairs in a list describing an object an interesting thing happens. To find out what this is, plot lines on graph paper connecting the following list of coordinates and then reverse them and plot the results of this too. What effect is achieved? (Hint: also draw on the plot a 45 degree line through the origin.) The list to use is (1,5), (3,3), (2,3), (3,4), (3,3).

6.2   Using the same list of points, change all the X values to −X. What happens to the drawing now? Try the same with −Y instead of Y. Then make both coordinates negative together. Have we discovered a way of mirroring computer drawings?

6.3   In what circumstances would polar coordinates as in Figure 6.6 be more useful than cartesian? Using polar coordinates, try plotting the following list of coordinates: (0,8), (30,8), (60,7), (90,6), (120,5), (150,4), (180,3), (210,2), (240,1), (270,0). Remember in this case the first of the coordinate pair is the angle in degrees, and the second distance from the origin. What do we have to do in order to make a more convincing spiral?

6.4   What would be the effect if you described a 3-D object in a left-handed coordinate system but your program assumed a right-handed one? How would you change from one system to another? Convince yourself that, by multiplying all the Z-values by −1, you can make a right-handed system into a left-handed one (and vice versa). Note that this change makes all negative Z-values positive and all positive ones negative. Is this the same as rotating the whole object about the Y-axis? In what way is it different?

6.5 Check the device coordinates of your graphic system. The information will be in the system manual and will probably be given in pixels. Some systems will allow you to choose from a range of resolutions. Note down all the possibilities.

6.6 Assume that you are an architect who wants to draw the plan of a building site which measures not more than 60 m × 40 m. You want this to be as big as it can be on a screen which has device coordinates of 240 m × 180 pixels. Work out a way to scale the site dimensions down to the correct size. Be sure to retain the correct proportions on the drawing.

6.7 Repeat Exercise 6.6 but this time for a site which is 600 m × 600 m. Still try to think of a way to make the drawing as large as possible whilst keeping the correct proportions of the site.

7

Modelling: 2-D Rectilinear Objects

When a 2-D object consists of straight lines such as the letter 'F' in Figure 6.5, we can describe it by listing the coordinates of its corners in an ordered fashion as we go round the perimeter. From the figure we can derive the following coordinate list:

(3,2), (3,7), (6,7), (6,6), (4,6), (4,5),
(5,5), (5,4), (4,4), (4,2), (3,2)

With this list, and the convention that we start at the first coordinate pair and proceed to draw lines between each pair until the end, we can easily reconstruct the letter. Note, though, that this is not the only line description we might have made. Even if we had kept the same coordinate values, we could have started with another pair or we could have proceeded anti-clockwise rather than clockwise. In addition, we might have used different units of measurement or set the letter in a different place in the coordinate system.

Because our coordinate list is related to a fixed origin throughout, this form is known as a set of *absolute coordinates*. Sometimes it is convenient to use *relative coordinates* where the origin of each line except the first is assumed to be the endpoint of its predecessor in the manner of Figure 7.1. Relative coordinates have their uses but cannot be manipulated in as flexible a way as the absolute variety.

Of course, to use the coordinate list in a program we need more information than just the list itself: we have to tell the computer what the numbers are for and how many pairs it is to deal with, either specifically or by means of some code which signals the end of

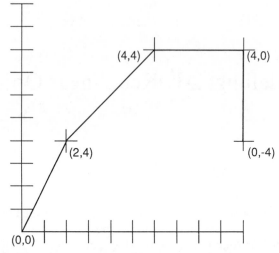

Figure 7.1   Relative coordinates where each point on a line is located
relative to its predecessor

the list – perhaps a pair of numbers such as 99999,99999 which are so
large that they cannot be mistaken for real coordinates.

If we use the first alternative, we can then store the description in
a 2-D array as in Table 7.1. The 2-D object description we have
given works for the good reason (known right back at least to Euclid
who lived about 2300 years ago) that you can only draw one straight
line between any two separate points. An additional bonus is that
the X- and Y-coordinates of all the points through which the line
passes are all related to one another by a simple formula, which is:

$$AX + BY + C = 0$$

Table 7.1

```
/* Load description array F(N,2) with coordinates of letter F */
Read N  /* Number of points */
Dim F(N,2)
For J = 1 to N
    Read F(J,1), F(J,2)
Next J
Data 11
Data 3,2,3,7,6,7,6,6,4,6,4,5
Data 5,5,5,4,4,4,4,2,3,2
```

This means that, if we know the coefficients A, B and C, we can calculate the proper value of Y for every X and vice versa. In addition, the formulation is useful for many other things such as calculating the angle of slope of the line or the point where two lines intersect (see Appendix 1).

Given two points with the coordinates (X1,Y1) and (X2,Y2), the coefficients A, B and C of the line joining them are found by the formulae:

$$A = Y2 - Y1$$
$$B = - (X2 - X1)$$
$$C = - (X1 * A + Y1 * B)$$

The AX + BY + C = 0 description is known as the *General Form of the Line*. The coefficients of the General Form of the Line which joins the points (1,1) and (5,3) can be arrived at by applying the above formulae as follows:

$$A = 3 - 1 = 2$$
$$B = -(5 - 1) = -4$$
$$C = -(1 * 2 + 1 * -4) = -(2 - 4) = 2$$

so that 2X − 4Y + 2 = 0 (or its simpler form, X − 2Y + 1 = 0) is the description. Checking the result by using the formulation:

$$X = 2Y - 1$$

we see that if Y = 1 then X = 1, and if Y = 3 then X = 5 which is what we expect. Additionally, if Y = 2 then X = 3, so that the point (3,2) is also on the line (as illustrated in Figure 7.2).

The General Form of the Line derives from conventional geometry in which any line is assumed to be of infinite length. Thus, as far as the General description is concerned, our line extends beyond the points (X1,Y1) and (X2,Y2) out into space in both directions. We see, for example, that if Y = 0 then X = −1 and if Y = 5 then X = 9, telling us that the line also passes through the points (−1,0) and (9,5) even though these are actually beyond the ends of our original line segment.

The idea of lines being infinitely long is troublesome in computer graphics and, if we need to restrict our description only to those points which actually lie between given end points, we need a different formulation – such as the so-called *Parametric Description*

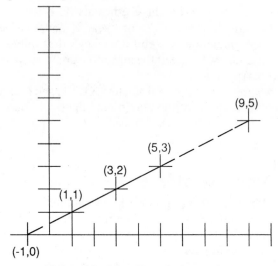

Figure 7.2   Line through given points

of the Line. Under this formulation, any point on the line joining the two points (X1,Y1) and (X2,Y2) has the coordinates:

$$X = X1 + t * (X2 - X1)$$
$$Y = Y1 + t * (Y2 - Y1)$$

where, if the points are to lie within the end points, t must run from 0 to 1 inclusive. Thus, all points lying on the line segment from (1,1) to (5,3) have the coordinates:

$$X = 1 + t * (5 - 1) = 1 + 4 * t$$
$$Y = 1 + t * (3 - 1) = 1 + 2 * t$$

providing that t lies between 0 and 1.

If t = 0 then we see that the coordinates are (1,1) and if t = 1 then the coordinates are (5,3), which is as expected. When t = 0.5 then the coordinates are (3,2), a point half way along the line. By rearranging the formula we see that

$$t = (X - 1) / 4 \text{ and}$$
$$t = (Y - 1) / 2$$

Using these formulae, we can check if the point $(-1,0)$ lies on our line. In this case:

$t = (-1 -1)/4 = -0.5$ and
$t = (0 - 1)/2 = -0.5$

But -0.5 is less than 0 and this fact shows that the point is not on the line segment (even though, as we already know, it is on the line continuation). Note that, if we obtain two different values of t for a point then, regardless of whether or not the values of t are between 0 and 1, the point does not lie on the line at all.

Both the General and the Parametric Forms are very useful in computer graphics and the reader would find it valuable to be familiar with them.

Other representations

The block letter 'F' is quite conveniently represented as a continuous list of coordinates arranged in an array. This is because we made it a simple, closed figure in which the end point of every line is the start point of the next. Other, more complicated, figures can also be described by means of a continuous line providing that they meet certain conditions. These are either:

1   That all points have an *even* number of lines running from them; or
2   That just two points have an *odd* number of lines running from them.

If the first condition holds then any point can be chosen as the start of the circuit. In the second case, only one of the odd points can be chosen. These rules make it clear that Figures 7.3a and 7.3b can be described by a continuous line but that Figure 7.3c cannot.

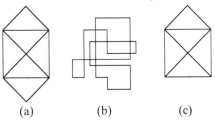

(a)   (b)   (c)

Figure 7.3   Only (a) and (b) can be drawn with a continuous line

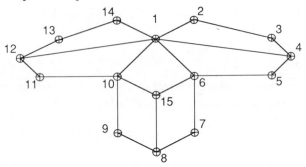

Figure 7.4 A company logo too complex to be drawn with one continuous line

Where it is not possible to meet the continuity conditions or where more complicated objects are required, another method of description might be more appropriate. For example, if we wish to describe the object shown in Figure 7.4 (which could be a company logo), a single list would not do because, in this case, there are four vertices which have an odd number of lines. Two options are open to us in describing such an object.

Firstly, we could divide it up into simpler objects which are themselves continuous, and then store the resulting parts in separate arrays. Our logo divides up in a number of different ways of which Figure 7.5 shows an example. If we list the coordinates of these figures, though, we see that some pairs are recorded two or three times. Indeed, although there are only 15 separate points in the figure, we have to have an array with 23 entries to accommodate

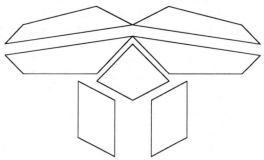

Figure 7.5 One possible subdivision of Figure 7.4

them. In more complicated cases, we might have even greater repetition and this could be very expensive in storage or could lead to errors in typing or editing the vastly increased numbers of duplicated coordinates. However, the most important defect of a description which duplicates the same point many times is that it slows up the essential task of transformation.

In the second option, we give each of the points a code number and record its coordinates. In addition, we make a separate list of the point numbers in the order in which they should be joined by lines. The points list can then be stored in a 2-D array as before, and the lines list can be held in a 1-D array. We might arrange this so that it holds both the point indexes and a count of the number of points it contains. The lists are as in Table 7.2.

Table 7.2

Point Coordinate List

Point	X	Y
1	0	2
2	2	3
3	6	2
4	7	1
5	6	0
6	2	0
7	2	-3
8	0	-4
9	-2	-3
10	-2	0
11	-6	0
12	-7	1
13	-6	2
14	-2	3
15	0	-1

Line list
5
1,12,13,14,1
14
1,2,3,4,5,6,7,8,9,10,11,12,1,4
6
8,15,10,1,6,15
0

Table 7.3

```
5
1,2,3,4,1
5
1,4,5,6,1
5
1,6,15,10,1
5
6,7,8,15,6
5
15,8,9,10,15
5
1,10,11,12,1
5
1,12,13,14,1
0
```

There are circumstances when even this description is inadequate. In particular, it is sometimes necessary to ensure that our line list separately describes all the polygons because we might want the computer to colour or shade them in. If this is the case, then the same point coordinate list will do, but our line list would have to read something like that outlined in Table 7.3. Here, the numbers on lines of their own indicate how many polygon vertices are to follow. As it happens, all the polygons in this figure have only four sides and are closed (with the last vertex being the same as the first), so we could reduce the data to the list of Table 7.4 and know that we could properly decode it. In the general case, however, we could not be sure that four-sided polygons would always be used nor that all of them would be closed. Thus, it is probably safest to write our description routine for the full data even though this occupies more space. Our points and line lists adequately describe the geometry of

Table 7.4

```
1,2,3,4,1
1,4,5,6,1
1,6,15,10,1
6,7,8,15,6
15,8,9,10,15
1,10,11,12,1
1,12,13,14,1
0
```

polygonal figures but more detail will be needed to deal with such things as line types, colour and shading.

Exercises

7.1 Show by manual plotting that the effect of subtracting three from each of the X-values of the letter 'F' coordinates is to move the figure three units to the left. What happens when you add five units to each of the X- and Y-coordinates? Plot the results of other additions and subtractions to confirm that, as long as we keep the same relationships between coordinates in the set, making differences in the actual numbers only changes the position of the figure.

7.2 Multiply each coordinate pair by a fixed number and plot the result. What happens now? Note that not only does the size of the figure change, but also its position.

7.3 Can you think of circumstances when relative coordinates might be more useful than absolute ones. Hint: how can we change size of a figure without changing its position?

7.4 Write a program to calculate the General Form of the Line joining two points. This program will be converted later to a subroutine. Use it to confirm the following results:

$(0,0)$ to $(5,5)$ $X - Y = 0$ (i.e. $A = 1, B = -1, C = 0$)
$(3,1)$ to $(2,7)$ $6X + Y - 19 = 0$ *or* $X + 0.167Y - 3.167 = 0$
$(4,6)$ to $(10,6)$ $-Y + 6 = 0$
$(-4.6,-32)$ to $(500,90.92)$ $122.92X - 504.6Y - 15581.8 = 0$
$\qquad\qquad\qquad\qquad\qquad$ *or* $X - 4.105Y - 126.764 = 0$

7.5 Use your program to check the following results:

$(0,0)$ to $(3,7)$ $A = 7, B = -3, C = 0$
$(0,0)$ to $(-3,7)$ $A = 7, B = 3, C = 0$
$(0,0)$ to $(-3,-7)$ $A = -7, B = 3, C = 0$
$(0,0)$ to $(3,-7)$ $A = -7, B = -3, C = 0$

What do you deduce from the pattern of these coefficients? Does what you deduce help you to explain why the only line which has a positive Y coefficient in Exercise 7.4 is the one from $(3,1)$ to $(2,7)$?

7.6 Confirm that, for the line from $(0,0)$ to $(3,7)$, if $X = 1$ then $Y = 2.333$ and if $X = 6$ then $Y = 14$.

7.7 Write a program (again to be used later as a subroutine) to compute the Parametric Description of the Lines for the following segments:

$(0,0)$ to $(5,5)$ $X = 5t$ and $Y = 5t$
$(3,1)$ to $(2,7)$ $X = 3 - t$ and $Y = 1 + 6t$
$(4,6)$ to $(10,6)$ $X = 4 + 6t$ and $Y = 6$
$(-4.6,-32)$ to $(500,90.92)$ $X = -4.6 + 504.6t$ and $Y = -32 + 122.92t$

7.8 Use the results of the previous exercise to check where the line $X = 150$ meets the line from $(-4.6, -32)$ to $(500, 90.92)$. You should get the answer:

$X = 150$ and $Y = 5.66$ (i.e. where $t = 0.3064$).

7.9 Show that $t = 1.333$ where the line $Y = 9$ crosses the line through $(3, 1)$ and $(2, 7)$. Confirm that the point of intersection lies outside the line segment $(3, 1)$ to $(2, 7)$ because $t > 1$.

8

Modelling: 2-D Curved Objects

We noted in the previous chapter that, as only one straight line can be drawn through two separate points, any straight line can be described simply by listing the coordinates of its endpoints. Curved lines, on the other hand, are quite different. Any number of curved lines can be drawn through two points, so more information is needed to describe objects made up of curves.

Figure 8.1   'Curved' line

However, most of the graphics devices we are likely to use can only draw curves as if they were made up of a large number of straight lines (or as a collection of illuminated pixels) as illustrated in Figure 8.1. When we are modelling curved objects, therefore, we have to give the computer the coordinates of the straight lines or points to use. For some shapes we have to do this directly by means of a list: many classes of curve, though, can be described by formulae from which the coordinates can be calculated. Circles and ellipses are one class where this is possible.

Circles and ellipses

The coordinates (X,Y) of all the points on a circle centred about (Xcentre, Ycentre) and whose radius is R are given by the formulae:

X = Xcentre + R * Cos (A)
Y = Ycentre + R * Sin (A)

where the angle A goes from 0 to 360 degrees (or from 0 to 2 * PI radians).

For these expressions to represent the sort of circle we draw with a pair of compasses, A should vary infinitesimally from angle to angle but, for most computer graphics purposes, it is sufficient for the angle to change in quite large steps – say of 5 degrees. Although this produces a polygon of 72 sides rather than a true circle, at reasonably small radii the figure appears curved enough to fool us into believing that we are seeing a true circle (Figure 8.2). For very small radii, even smaller numbers of sides produce acceptable results.

Programs using the simple formulae given work quite quickly even though they have to compute a new sine and cosine at every step. We can improve on this performance, though, by using a mathematical trick made possible by the formulae for the sine and cosine of sums of angles.

For the two angles A and DA, these are:

Cos (A + DA) = Cos (A) * Cos (DA) − Sin (A) * Sin (DA)
Sin (A + DA) = Sin (A) * Cos (DA) + Cos (A) * Sin (DA)

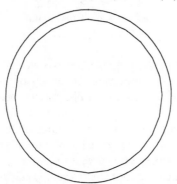

Figure 8.2   Circles of 24 and 72 sides

By using these formulae, we can remove the necessity for the continued recalculation of the sine and cosine functions. To do this we devise a *recursive* relationship where the values of X and Y at one point are used to calculate the values at the adjoining point. The equations to achieve this are:

$$X(I) = Xcentre + R * Cos(A)$$
$$Y(I) = Ycentre + R * Sin(A)$$
$$X(I + 1) = Xcentre + R * Cos(A + DA)$$
$$Y(I + 1) = Ycentre + R * Sin(A + DA)$$

After some algebraic manipulation of the second pair of equations and the use of the sums of angles formulae, we arrive at:

$$X(I + 1) = Xcentre + (X(I)-Xcentre) * Cos(DA) - (Y(I) - Ycentre) * Sin(DA)$$
$$Y(I + 1) = Ycentre + (X(I) - Xcentre) * Sin(DA) + (Y(I) - Ycentre) * Cos(DA)$$

These equations describe each point using only the angle DA. Starting the circle at A = 0 and I = 1, we then have:

$$X(1) = Xcentre + R$$
$$Y(1) = Ycentre$$

Then, by setting the angle DA to a constant value, we can calculate the sine and cosine functions of DA just once and use the same results throughout. A subroutine like that in Table 8.1 would generate the coordinates of a circle very quickly.

Table 8.1 *Circle* subroutine

```
Subroutine Circle (Num, Xcentre, Ycentre, Radius; N, Outarray)
Integer Num, N
Real Xcentre, Ycentre, Radius, Outarray
/* Loads Outarray with the coordinates of a circle centred at
(Xcentre, Ycentre). The circle is approximated by a polygon of Num sides */
Local Integer J
Local Real DA, C, S, Xdiff, Ydiff
    N = Num + 1
    Dim Outarray (N,2)
    DA = 360 / Num        /* assumes degrees */
    C = Cos (DA)
    S = Sin (DA)
```

```
    Outarray (1,1) = Xcentre + Radius       /* first point */
    Outarray (1,2) = Ycentre
    For J = 2 to Num                        /* intermediate points */
        Xdiff = Outarray (J-1,1) - Xcentre
        Ydiff = Outarray (J-1,2) - Ycentre
        Outarray (J,1) = Xcentre + Xdiff * C - Ydiff * S
        Outarray (J,2) = Ycentre + Xdiff * S + Ydiff * C
    Next J
    Outarray (N,1) = Outarray (1,1)         /* last point */
    Outarray (N,2) = Outarray (1,2)
End of Circle subroutine
```

As the remark in the code says, the subroutine assumes that our computer can work in degrees, but not all systems have this facility and most can only work in radians. If this is the case, change the lines:

$$C = Cos\ (DA)$$
$$S = Sin\ (DA)$$

to read

F = PI / 180 / * degrees to radians conversion * /
$$C = Cos\ (DA * F)$$
$$S = Sin\ (DA * F)$$

Many of the problems beginners encounter with curve drawing and use of angles arise because they forget that their system uses radians rather than degrees. You will probably find it better to work with radians in the body of your subroutines even if you want your input and output to be in degrees. This is the method we will use in this book. Radians are converted to degrees by multiplying them by $180/\pi$.

It will not have escaped your notice that the same subroutine will deal with the well-known regular polygons (triangles, squares, pentagons and so on) if the value of Num is set sufficiently low. Ellipses can be described by a centre point and two other parameters known as major and minor axes, which we will think of as Radius1 and Radius2 (Figure 8.3). Table 8.2 gives a subroutine to deal with ellipses (and with circles too if we set Radius1 = Radius2).

Note that for efficiency, especially in cases where many circles or ellipses have to be described, it is probably best to begin your

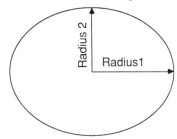

Figure 8.3   Ellipse showing major and minor axes

graphics program by storing the coordinates of a circle of radius = 1 centred at (0,0): a unit circle. When particular instances of circles are needed, it is only necessary then to scale the unit circle coordinates to the right size (by multiplying them by the radius) and to translate the centre to the correct position by additon or subtrac-

Table 8.2   *Ellipse* subroutine

```
Subroutine Ellipse (Num, Xcentre, Ycentre, Rds1, Rds2; N, Outarray)
Integer Num, N
Real Xcentre, Ycentre, Rds1, Rds2, Outarray
/* Loads Outarray with the coordinates of an ellipse centred at
(Xcentre, Ycentre). The ellipse has a major axis of Rds1 and a minor axis of
Rds2. It is approximated by a polygon of Num sides */
Local Integer J
Local Real DA, F, C, S
   N = Num + 1
   Dim Outarray (N,2)
   DA = 360 / Num                       /* assumes degrees */
   Outarray (1,1) = Xcentre + Rds1           /* first point */
   Outarray (1,2) = Ycentre
   F = Pi / 180
   For J = 2 to Num                  /* intermediate points */
      C = Cos (DA * F)
      S = Sin (DA * F)
      Outarray (J,1) = Xcentre + Rds1 * C
      Outarray (J,2) = Ycentre + Rds2 * S
   Next J
   Outarray (N,1) = Outarray (1,1)              /* last point */
   Outarray (N,2) = Outarray (1,2)
End of Ellipse subroutine
```

tion. Ellipses can be dealt with by separately scaling the X- and Y-coordinates of the unit circle according to Radius1 and Radius2. The unit circle can be described by a subroutine like that in Table 8.3.

Table 8.3   *Unitcircle* subroutine

```
Subroutine Unitcircle (Num; N, Outarray)
Integer Num, N
Real Outarray
/* Loads Outarray with the coordinates of a circle, radius = 1, centred at
(0,0). The circle is approximated by a polygon of Num sides */
Local Integer J
Local Real DA, F, C, S, Xdiff, Ydiff
    N = Num + 1
    Dim Outarray (N,2)
    F = Pi / 180
    DA = 360 / Num                          /* assumes degrees */
    C = Cos (DA)
    S = Sin (DA)
    Outarray (1,1) = 1                      /* first point */
    Outarray (1,2) = 0
    For J = 2 to Num                        /* intermediate points */
        Xdiff = Outarray (J-1,1)
        Ydiff = Outarray (J-1,2)
        Outarray (J,1) = Xcentre + Xdiff * C - Ydiff * S
        Outarray (J,2) = Ycentre + Xdiff * S + Ydiff * C
    Next J
    Outarray (N,1) = 1                      /* last point */
    Outarray (N,2) = 0
End of Unitcircle subroutine
```

Arcs of circles

Often we need to describe only parts of circles and we can use a modification of the Circle subroutine to do this as in Table 8.4.

Table 8.4   *Arc* subroutine

```
Subroutine Arc (Num, Xc, Yc, Startangle, Arcangle, Rds; N, Outarray)
Integer Num, N
Real Xc, Yc, Startangle, Arcangle, Rds, Outarray
/* Loads Outarray with the coordinates of an arc centred at (Xc, Yc) and
radius = Rds running from Startangle to Startangle + Arcangle. The angles
```

are in degrees. Arcangle is negative for clockwise description and positive for anticlockwise. The arc is part of a circle approximated by a polygon of Num sides */

Local Integer J
Local Real DA, F, SA, AA, EA, C, S, Xdiff, Ydiff
   F = Pi / 180
   SA = Startangle * F
   AA = Arcangle * F
   DA = 360 / Num   /* assumes degrees */
/* N is the number of points in a slightly longer arc */
   N = **Int** ((**Abs** (AA) * 1.01) / DA)
   DA = DA * **Sgn** (AA) * F   /* to make sure DA is in correct direction */
   Dim Outarray (N,2)
   C = Cos (DA)
   S = Sin (DA)
   Outarray (1,1) = Xc + Rds * Cos (SA)   /* first point */
   Outarray (1,2) = Yc + Rds * Sin (SA)
   For J = 2 to N - 1   /* intermediate points */
      Xdiff = Outarray (J-1,1) - Xc
      Ydiff = Outarray (J-1,2) - Yc
      Outarray (J,1) = Xcentre + Xdiff * C - Ydiff * S
      Outarray (J,2) = Ycentre + Xdiff * S + Ydiff * C
   Next J
   EA = SA + AA
   Outarray (N,1) = Xc + Rds * Cos (EA)   /* last point */
   Outarray (N,2) = Yc + Rds * Sin (EA)
End of Arc subroutine

Circles through three points

The circle and arc routines we have given assume that we already know the centres and radii of curves as well as how much of them we are to draw. In practice, this knowledge is not always directly available. However, if we know three separate points through which a circle passes, we can calculate the radius and coordinates of the centre by means of the Three-pt-circle subroutine given in Table 8.5. This works by calculating the intersection point of the two perpendicular bisectors of the lines (X1,Y1) to (X2,Y2) and (X2, Y2) to (X3, Y3) as shown in Figure 8.4. For this reason, the points must be arranged in the order (X1,Y1), (X2,Y2), (X3,Y3) and must not be in a straight line – a condition known as *colinearity*. A check

Table 8.5　*Three-pt-circle* subroutine

Subroutine Three-pt-circle (X1, Y1, X2, Y2, X3, Y3; Xcntr, Ycntr, Radius)
Real X1, X2, X3, Y1, Y2, Y3, Xcntr, Ycntr, Radius
/* Calculates the centre and radius of a circle passing through the points
(X1,Y1), (X2,Y2), (X3,Y3) taken in order */
Local Real D1, D2, D3, D4, XX, YY, F1, F2
　　D1 = X2 - X1
　　D2 = Y2 - Y1
　　D3 = X3 - X1
　　D4 = Y3 - Y1
　　XX = X1 * X1
　　YY = Y1 * Y1
/* Calculate midpoints of lines */
　　F1 = (XX - X2 * X2 + YY - Y2 * Y2) * 0.5
　　F2 = (XX - X3 * X3 + YY - Y3 * Y3) * 0.5
/* Insert your test for colinearity here */
　　Ycntr = (D1 * F2 - D3 * F1) / (D3 * D2 - D1 * D4)
　　Xcntr = - (F1 + D2 * Ycntr) / D1
　　XX = (X1 - Xcntr) * (X1 - Xcntr)
　　YY = (Y1 - Ycntr) * (Y1 - Ycntr)
　　Radius = Sqr (XX + YY)
End of Three-pt-circle subroutine

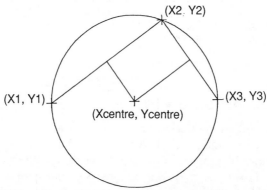

Figure 8.4　Three-point circle

should be inserted in the routine to ensure that the points are not
colinear and that they are separate. This is left as an exercise.

To create the coordinates of a circle passing through the points
(10,0), (10,6) and (4,12), we use the Three-pt-circle and then the
Circle subroutines as in Table 8.6.

Table 8.6

```
/* Program fragment using Circle */
Call Three-pt-circle (10, 0, 10, 6, 4, 12; X, Y, R)
Call  Circle (72, X, Y, R; Carray)
/* End of program fragment */
```

Alternatively, we can use the Three-pt-circle and the Unitcircle subroutines, as in Table 8.7. The latter is probably speedier if a number of different circles are to be drawn. In that case, the conversion of the unit circle coordinates should also be made into a subroutine.

Table 8.7

```
/* Program fragment using Unitcircle */
Call Unitcircle (72; Oarray)
    .    .    .
Call Three-pt-circle (10, 0, 10, 6, 4, 12; X, Y, R)
/* Convert the unit circle coordinates */
For J = 1 to 72
    Carray (J,1) = Oarray (J,1) * R + X
    Carray (J,2) = Oarray (J,2) * R + Y
Next J
/* End of program fragment */
```

For arcs of circles we need to know not only the centres and radii but also the starting angle and the angular measure of the arc. Given that point (XS,YS) represents the start and point (XE,YE) represents the end of the arc as shown in Figure 8.5, we can calculate these angles by means of the following formulae which use the Arctan trigonometrical function:

Startangle = Arctan ((YS − YC) / (XS − XC))
Endangle = Arctan ((YE − YC) / (XE − XC))

Arctan (X) is the angle whose Tangent is X; it is sometimes called ATAN or ATN in computer languages and usually returns its values in radians. A complication exists because ATAN functions only work for angles in the range −PI/2 to PI/2 (−90 degrees to 90 degrees) in the manner of Figure 8.6. This means that a simple call to the function will not always provide the correct answer and its results must be adjusted to suit the actual case. Assuming that we

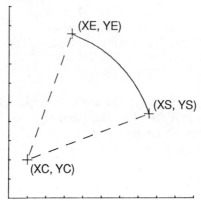

Figure 8.5   Arc drawing

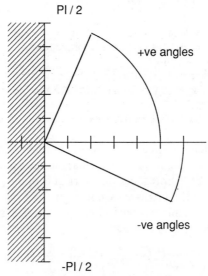

Figure 8.6   Arctangents

need the angle between the horizontal axis and a line from point (XC,YC) to (X,Y), the adjustments we have to make are included in Table 8.8.

One additional adjustment is needed to allow us to specify arcs in either clockwise or anticlockwise directions. We must ensure that our start angle is greater than the end angle for clockwise arcs and

Table 8.8 *Anglecalc* subroutine

```
Subroutine Anglecalc(XC, YC, X, Y, Flag; A)
Integer Flag
Real XC, YC, X, Y, A
/* Calculates the value of angle (in degrees if Flag = 0 and radians if Flag
= 1) between horizontal axis and a line from (XC,YC) to (X,Y) */
Local Real DX, DY
    If X = XC Then
        If Y > YC Then
            A = Pi / 2
        Else
            A = 3 * Pi / 2
        Endif
    Else
        DX = XC - X
        DY = YC - Y
        A = Arctan (DY / DX)
    Endif
/* Make any adjustments to A */
    If X > XC And Y < YC Then
        A = A + 2 * Pi
    Else
        If X < XC Then
            A = A + Pi
        Endif
    Endif
/* If result needed in degrees, perform conversion */
    If Flag Then
        A = A * 180 / Pi
    Endif
End of Anglecalc subroutine
```

less than it is for arcs in the opposite direction. Thus a subroutine to determine the centre, radius and angles of a three-point arc could be of the form given in Table 8.9. This routine makes use of the Arcos function where Arcos (A) is the angle whose Cosine is A. You may find that your system does not provide this function. However, it can be derived from the Arctan function by the formula:

$$\text{Arcos}(X) = -\text{Arctan}(X / \text{Sqr}(-X * X + 1)) + 1.570796$$

This gives the result in radians and assumes that Arctan is in radians.

Table 8.9   *Tparcinfo* subroutine

Subroutine Tparcinfo(Xstart, Ystart, Xmid, Ymid, Xend, Yend, Flag;
XC, YC, R, SA, AA)
Integer Flag
Real Xstart, Ystart, Xmid, Ymid, Xend, Yend, XC, YC, R, SA, AA
/* Determines the centre (XC,YC), radius R, start angle SA, and extent of
angle AA, of an arc passing through 3 points given in order. Angles are in
degrees if Flag = 1 or radians if Flag = 0 */
Local Integer J
Local Real D1, D2, D3, D4, D9, D0, A, B, C, US, VS, UM, VM, UE,
VE, T, F1, F2, F3, A0, B0, C0, Q, X, Y, CS, SI
/* First, calculate the centre point and radius* /
   Call Three-pt-circle (Xstart, Ystart, Xmid, Ymid, Xend, Yend; XC, YC, R)
   D1 = Xmid - Xstart
   D2 = Ymid - Ystart
   D3 = Xend - Xstart
   D4 = Yend - Ystart
   D9 = Xmid - Xend
   D0 = Ymid - Yend
   J = 10000   /* a factor to help in testing */
   A = Sqr (D9 * D9 + D0 * D0) /* length A */
   B = Sqr (D1 * D1 + D2 * D2) /* length B */
   C = Sqr (D3 * D3 + D4 * D4) /* length C */
/* Shift the points to the origin */
   US = Xstart - XC
   VS = Ystart - YC
   UE = Xend - XC
   VE = Yend - YC
   UM = Xmid - XC
   VM = Ymid - YC
   T = 2 * R * R
   If B >= C **Or** A > = C **Then**
      F3 = (T - C * C) / T
      C0 = Arcos (F3)
      Q = C0 - 2 * Pi
/* Check direction of arc by rotating start point clockwise and checking
its relation with endpoint */
      CS = Cos (C0)
      SI =Sin (C0)
      X = **Int** ((US * CS - VS * SI) * J)
      Y = **Int** ((US * SI + VS * CS) * J)
   If Int (UE *J) **And Int** (VE * J) **Then**
      AA = Q

```
      Else
         AA = -Q
      End if
   Else
      F1 = (T - B * B) / T
      BO = Arcos (F1)
      F2 = (T - A * A) / T
      AO = Arcos (F2)
      Q = AO + BO
/* Check direction of arc with midpoint */
      CS = Cos (BO)
      SI = Sin (BO)
      X = Int ((US * CS - VS * SI) * J)
      Y = Int ((US * SI + VS * CS) * J)
      If X = Int (UM * J) And Y = Int (VM * J) Then
         AA = Q
      Else
         AA = -Q
      Endif
   Endif
   Call Anglecalc (XC, YC, Xstart, Ystart, 0; SA)
/* If you want angles in degrees, perform conversion */
   If Flag Then
      AA = AA * 180 / Pi
      SA = SA * 180 / Pi
   Endif
End of Tparcinfo subroutine
```

In a working system, we would probably combine the Three-pt-circle and the Tparcinfo subroutines together into one routine, perhaps called Circinfo. A circle or an arc would be returned depending on the setting of the first parameter. Thus:

Circinfo (0, 10, 0, 10, 6, 4, 12, Flg; XC, YC, R, SA, EA) where the parameter is 0, would return details of a circle through the points (10,0), (10,6), (4,12), whilst:

Circinfo (1, 10, 0, 10, 6, 4, 12, Flg; XC, YC, R, SA, EA) where the parameter is 1, would return details of an arc starting at (10,0) and ending at (4,12). You would then call the appropriate circle or arc routine using this information for the parameters.

Tangent lines and arcs

A problem in creating drawings made up of lines and arcs of circles such as those in Figures 8.7a and 8.7b is working out the centres of the circles and their points of contact with the lines. This is particularly so when we want the lines to flow smoothly into the arcs in the manner of Figure 8.7a. In order to achieve this smoothness and continuity, we must ensure that the lines are *tangents* to the arcs; in

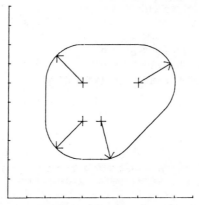

Figure 8.7a   Lines and arcs 1

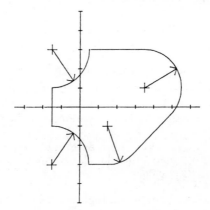

Figure 8.7b   Lines and arcs 2

other words, that they meet the arcs at points where the lines and the radii are at right angles (Figure 8.8). These points are known as

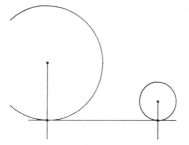

Figure 8.8 Tangent points

tangent points. We can use the formulae of conventional coordinate geometry to work out the tangent points and lines but, from the point of view of computer graphics, this gives rise to a complication which can be illustrated if we consider drawing a line which is tangential to two circles. As can be seen from Figure 8.9, there are, in fact, four possible tangent lines which connect the circles. We have to have a method of describing which of these possibilities we mean.

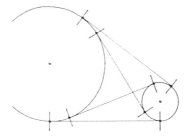

Figure 8.9 Tangent lines

We can do this by introducing the concept of directionality into our lines and arcs. Looking at Figure 8.10, we can see that the line in Figure 8.10a can be thought of as a continuation of Circle 2 drawn anticlockwise to Circle 1 also drawn anticlockwise. By similar reasoning, the line in Figure 8.10b is the continuation of Circle 1 drawn anticlockwise to Circle 2 drawn anticlockwise; the line in Figure 8.10c is the continuation of Circle 1 drawn anticlockwise to Circle 2 drawn clockwise; and the line in Figure 8.10d is the continuation of Circle 2 drawn clockwise to Circle 1 drawn anticlockwise. (There are other possible combinations of directionality but, if you examine them as an exercise, you will see that they duplicate the cases given.)

To indicate the directionality of our arcs and lines, we will introduce the convention that an arc with a positive value for its radius must be drawn anticlockwise and one with a negative value must be drawn clockwise. The direction of a line segment is given by the order in which its endpoints are listed. A subroutine to compute the tangent points using this convention is given in Table 8.10.

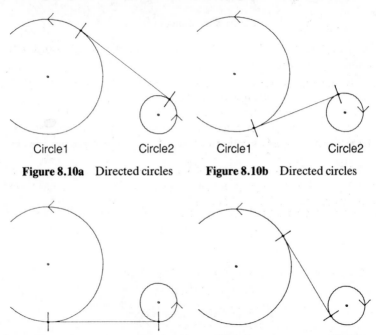

Circle1　　　　Circle2　　　　Circle1　　　　Circle2

Figure 8.10a　Directed circles　　　**Figure 8.10b**　Directed circles

Circle1　　　　Circle2　　　　Circle1　　　　Circle2

Figure 8.10c　Directed circles　　　**Figure 8.10d**　Directed circles

Table 8.10　*Twocirctan* subroutine

Subroutine Twocirctan (X1, Y1, R1, X2, Y2, R2; XP, YP, XQ, YQ)
Real X1, X2, XP, XQ, Y1, Y2, YP, YQ, R1, R2
/* Returns the coordinates of the points (XP,YP) and (XQ,YQ) of a tangent line to the circles with centres (X1,Y1) and (X2,Y2). The order in which the circles are given and the signs of the radii are important. Based on a

technique devised at the Department of Computer Science, Lubljana, Yugoslavia */

Local Real DX, DY, DL, D1, D2, F, FF, FO, F1, F2, JX , JY

```
 DX = X2 - X1   /* the vector D from centre to centre */
 DY = Y2 - Y1
 JX = -DY       /* the vector J at right angles to D */
 JY = DX
 DL = Sqr (DX * DX + DY * DY )   /* length of D */
 F = (R1 - R2) / DL
 FF = F *F
 FO = Sqr (1 - FF)
 F1 = R1 / DL
 F2 = R2 / DL
 D1 = F * DX - FO * JX
 D2 = F * DY - FO * JY
 XP = X1 + F1 * D1
 YP = Y1 + F1 * D2
 XQ = X2 + F2 * D1
 YQ = Y2 + F2 * D2
```

End of Twocirctan subroutine

In order to describe a shape like that in Figure 8.11, we would create the anticlockwise arcs and lines from P1 to P2 and P3 to P4 in a program fragment like that in Table 8.11.

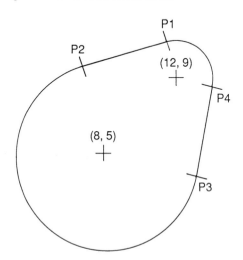

Figure 8.11   Shape made of directed lines and arcs

Table 8.11

```
/* Program fragment to load array Out3 with the coordinates
of Figure 8.11 */
/*First calculate points P1 and P2 */
   Call Twocirctan (12, 9, 2, 8, 5, 5; XP1, YP1, XP2, YP2)
/* Calculate points P3 and P4 */
   Call Twocirctan (8, 5, 5, 12, 9, 2; XP3, YP3, XP4, YP4)
/* Calculate angles for Arc1 and Arc2 */
   Call Anglecalc (12, 9, XP4-12, YP4-9, 1; SA1)
   Call Anglecalc (12, 9, XP1-12, YP1-9, 1; EA1)
   Call Anglecalc (8, 5, XP2-8, YP2-5, 1; SA2)
   Call Anglecalc (8, 5, XP3-8, YP2-5, 1; EA2)
/* Describe Arc1 and Arc2 with positive radii */
   Call Arc (72, 12, 9, SA1, SA1 + EA1, 2; N1, Out1)
   Call Arc (72, 8, 5, SA2, SA2 + EA2, 5; N2, Out2)
/* Load array Out3*/
   N3 = N1 + N2 + 1
   J = 0
   Dim Out3 (N3,2)
   For K= 1 to N1
      J = J + 1
      Out3 (J,1) = Out1 (K,1)
      Out3 (J,2) = Out1 (K,2)
   Next K
   For K = 1 to N2
      J = J + 1
      Out3 (J,1) = Out2 (K,1)
      Out3 (J,2) = Out2 (K,2)
   Next K
   Out3(N3,1) = Out1(1,1)
   Out3(N3,2) = Out1(1,2)
/* End of program fragment */
```

Polynomial curves

Curves of freer form than circles or ellipses have to be described in
more complicated ways. If we have a digitiser and an existing
drawing of an object, we can trace the outline in point mode making
our points as close together as seems appropriate. Tracing the exact
points on free-flowing curves, however, is not an easy task because

bumps, depressions and other discrepancies inevitably creep in to spoil the outline. A number of techniques have been devised to help minimise these discrepancies. These techniques allow us simply to select a few pertinent points and to calculate the curve from them.

Two basic methods of doing this are possible. In the first, we choose points through which we want the curve to pass (Figure 8.12a). In the second, we choose points which, though not all lying on the curve itself, are used to control its shape (Figure 8.12b). Both

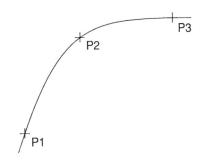

Figure 8.12a   Points on a curve

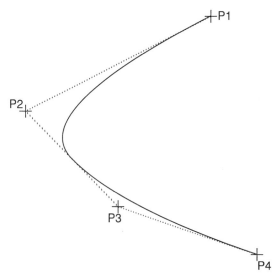

Figure 8.12b   Control points off curve

methods are useful and have their applications. The second is perhaps the most popular in computer aided design where curves are often created interactively and blended with others to produce an aesthetically pleasing result.

When we want a curve to pass through a number of points, it is useful to remember that any N points can be smoothly connected by a polynomial of degree N−1. That is to say, three points can be joined by a curve of the form:

$$Y = K3 \cdot X^2 + K2 \cdot X + K1$$

which is a polynomial of degree 2; four points can be joined by a curve of the form:

$$Y = K4 \cdot X^3 + K3 \cdot X^2 + K2 \cdot X + K1$$

which is a polynomial of degree 3, and so on.

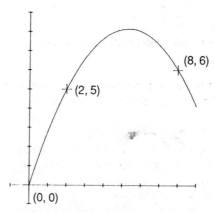

Figure 8.13a   Polynomial: degree 2

So, given the points (0,0), (2,5) and (8,6), we can use the techniques of conventional algebra to work out that they all lie on the curve shown in Figure 8.13a and given by the polynomial:

$$Y = -0.29166 \cdot X^2 + 3.0833 \cdot X$$

where K3 = −0.29166 and K2 = 3.0833. (K1 = 0 because the curve passes through the origin.) Unfortunately, the curves that result from application of this simple method are not always the ones that seem intuitively to fit the bill. It may be thought, for example, that the curve in Figure 8.13a reaches too high a level between points (2,5) and (8,6). To deal with this, we can add an extra point between

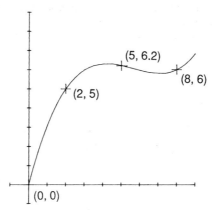

Figure 8.13b   Polynomial: degree 3

the two, say at (5,6.2), and fit a new polynomial of degree 3 to the set of four points. Specifically, the cubic polynomial,

$$Y = 0.42778 \cdot X^3 - 0.719446 \cdot X^2 + 3.76778 \cdot X$$

will work. This produces the curve shown in Figure 8.13b, which is certainly flatter than the other but now has a slight wave introduced into it. The waviness is a characteristic of straightforward polynomial curves – indeed the higher the degree, the more waves tend to appear. Furthermore, you will note that, at the point (8,6), the curve of degree 2 is sloping sharply downwards and that of degree 3, slightly upwards. As we often want curves to blend with given straight lines or other curves, simple polynomial fitting is clearly not enough. However, if we know the slopes of the lines we want to blend with at the end of the curves we can use these to add further information to our curve-fitting procedure. With the start and endpoints plus the slopes, we can fit a polynomial of degree 3 and, if we also know a point lying between the two end points, we can fit a polynomial of degree 4.

The slope of a line is calculated by taking any two points (X1,Y1) and (X2,Y2) on the line and using the formula:

Slope = (Y2 − Y1) / (X2 − X1).

When Y2 = Y1, the slope is 0 because the line is horizontal. When X2 = X1, the slope is infinite because the line is vertical.

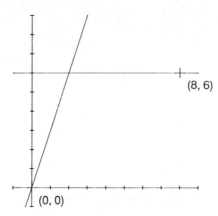

Figure 8.14

From Figure 8.14 we can see that line 1 has a slope of 3 and line 2 has a slope of 0. We will use these slopes and Subroutine Polyfit to pass a curve through the points (0,0) and (8,6). Subroutine Polyfit will compute the coordinates of the curve which passes through two or three points and has given start and end slopes (Table 8.12).

Table 8.12 *Polyfit* subroutine

Subroutine Polyfit (Num, XS, YS, SS, XE, YE, ES, XM, YM, Inc; N, OA)
Integer Num, N
Real XS, XE, XM, YS, YE, YM, SS, ES, Inc, OA
/* Loads OA with the N pairs of coordinates of a polynomial of degree 3 fitted through Num = 2 points, or degree 4 fitted through Num = 3 points. SS and ES are the slopes of the lines at the start and ends of the curve. (XM,YM) is the intermediate point. Inc is the desired increment in the X − direction. The array K holds the KN coefficients of the polynomial. If these are needed outside the subroutine, they should be included as return parameters */

```
Local Integer KN, K9,J
Local Real XX, X1, B1,B2, B3, H, HH, HT, S
   XX = XE - XS
   N = Int (Abs (XX / Inc)) + 1
   KN = 5
   Dim OA (N,2), K (KN)
/* Compute coefficients */
   K(1) = YS
   K(2) = SS * XX
   If Num = 2 Then
      XM = 0
      YM = 0
   Endif
   H = (XM - XS) / XX
   HH = H * H
   B1 = YE - YS - K(2)
   B2 = XX * ES- K(2)
   If Num = 3 Then
      B3 = YM - YS - K(2) * H
      H3 = HH * (HH - 2 * H + 1)
      K(5) = (B3 - B1 * HH - HH * (H -1) * ( B2 - 2 * B1))) / H3
   Else
      B3 = YM - YS
      K(5) = 0
      KN = 4
   Endif
   K(4) = B2 - 2 * B1 - 2 * K(5)
   K(3) = YE - YS - K(2) - K(4) - K(5)
   HT = XS - Inc
/* Compute coordinates from coefficients */
   For J = 1 to N
      S = K(1)
      HT = Ht + Inc
      X1 = (HT - XS) / XX
      For K9 =1 to 4
         S = S + K(K9 +1) * X1 ** K9
      Next K9
      OA(J,1) = HT
      OA(J,2) = S
   Next J
End of Polyfit Subroutine
```

Thus, a fourth degree polynomial of the form:

$$Y = 19.5555 \cdot Xd^4 - 27.111 \cdot Xd^3 - 10.4444 \cdot Xd^2 + 24 \cdot Xd$$

will fit the three points (0,0), (2,5) and (8,6) but, again, goes rather high before flattening out (Figure 8.15a). Note that, unlike in the previous case where X was the actual value of the horizontal displacement, here Xd takes the value of $X/(XS - XE)$ so that the X-parameter lies in the range 0 to 1.

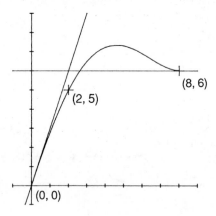

Figure 8.15a

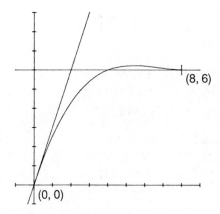

Figure 8.15b

The third degree polynomial:

$$Y = 12 \cdot Xd^3 - 30 \cdot Xd^2 + 24 \cdot Xd$$

fitted to (0,0) and (8,6) behaves quite well (Figure 8.15b). However, if we can set the intermediate point at will, we can control the shape and obtain a fourth degree polynomial of the form:

$$Y = -7.5378 \cdot Xd^4 + 27.0756 \cdot Xd^3 - 37.5378 \cdot Xd^2 + 24 \cdot Xd$$

which passes through the intermediate point (3,5) and blends the lines in the required manner (Figure 8.15c).

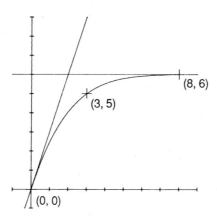

Figure 8.15c

There are a large number of other methods of drawing curves which pass through given points. Probably the most economical way of ensuring that a curve looks right is to divide it into relatively small sections and fit a polynomial of low degree with given end slopes to each part. For this to work we have to ensure that the end slope of one section is the same as the start slope of the next and that we have a free intermediate point to control the shape. This combination of requirements, together with the need in computer graphics and CAD to design objects with pleasing forms, has led to the technique of using parametric cubic curves with controlling points.

Parametric cubic curves

We learned in Chapter 7 that a straight line between points (X1,Y1) and (X2,Y2) can be described in terms of a single parameter, t, and the formulae:

$$X = X1 + t * (X2 - X1)$$
$$Y = Y1 + t * (Y2 - Y1)$$

where t runs from 0 to 1. We can combine these into a single parametric equation of the form:

$$P(t) = P1 + t * (P2 - P1)$$

if we assume that P1 is the vector (X1,Y1) and P2 is the vector (X2,Y2). This is a convenient shorthand description particularly when we realise that the parametric form also works for lines in three dimensions. That is to say,

$$Z = Z1 + t * (Z2 - Z1)$$

is also true for the line from (X1,Y1,Z1) to (X2,Y2,Z2). Examining the parametric description we can see that, as we travel along the line from t = 0 towards t = 1, the effect of P2 comes more and more into play. At t = 0, P2 has no influence; at t = 1, P2 dominates; at t = 0.5, P1 and P2 play equal parts, and so on.

We can use a similar technique to describe curved lines but we need to take into account the influence of more than two points. Also, in the case of a line, the influence of the points is directly proportional to the value of t. For curves, more complex relationships are needed and these are embodied in what are known as *blending functions*. Computer graphics workers have suggested many different blending functions and the literature abounds with a bewildering variety of methods which use them.

One of the most useful of these is due to Harry Timmer of the Douglas Aircraft Company who, in common with many others, uses four points (P1, P2, P3, P4) together with four blending functions (F1, F2, F3, F4) to describe curves parametrically. His formulation is:

$$P(t) = F1(t) \cdot P1 + F2(t) \cdot P2 + F3(t) \cdot P3 + F4(t) \cdot P4$$

and the particular blending functions he suggests are:

$$F1(t) = (1 - 2 \cdot t) \cdot (1 - t)^2$$
$$F2(t) = 4 \cdot t \cdot (1 - t)^2$$
$$F3(t) = 4 \cdot t^2 \cdot (1 - t)$$
$$F4(t) = (2 \cdot t - 1) \cdot t^2$$

For all points on the curve, t runs from 0 to 1 and, as can be seen, when t = 0, the first blending function becomes 1 and all the others 0, showing that only the first point has any influence on the curve.

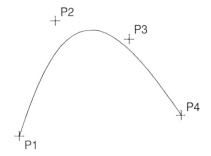

Figure 8.16a   Cubic fit

When t = 1, the last function becomes 1 and all the others 0, showing that only P4 has any effect. For intermediate values of t, each function and, hence, each point influences the shape. As Figure 8.16a indicates, only the points P1 and P4 are actually on the curve: the other two are situated at some distance from it and are there to control its shape. If we join the four points with straight lines as in Figure 8.16b, we see that the curve is tangent to line P1–P2 at the point P1, and tangent to the line P3–P4 at the point P4.

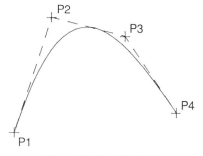

Figure 8.16b   Cubic fit

In addition, and this is the characteristic of Timmer's variation, the curve either touches or crosses the line P2–P3 at its midpoint. If the line P1–P4 is parallel to P2–P3, then the curve is also tangent to P2–P3 at the midpoint. The procedure can be put into a subroutine (Table 8.13).

Complex shapes, including closed curves, are built up from sets of four-point lines as shown in Figure 8.17. The arrangement of the bounding lines ensures that individual curves properly blend into

Table 8.13　*Cubicfit* subroutine

```
Subroutine Cubicfit (Num, Parray; N, Oarray)
Integer Num, N
Real Parray, Oarray
/* Uses Timmer's method to fit a parametric cubic curve using the four
points whose coordinates are in Parray of dimension (4,2). The coordinates
of the curve are put into Oarray of dimension (N,2). The value of Num sets
the number of steps in the final curve */
Local Integer Count, K
Local Real A1, A2, F, T, TT, T1,T2
    N = Num + 1
    Dim F (4), Oarray (N,2)
    For Count = 1 to N
        T = (1 / Num) * (Count - 1)
        TT = T * T
        T1 = 1 - T
        T2 = T1 * T1
/* Calculate the blending functions */
        F(1) = (1 - 2 * T) * T2
        F(2) = 4 * T * T2
        F(3) = 4 * TT * T1
        F(4) = (2 * T -1) * TT
        A1 = 0
        A2 = 0
/* Calculate the coordinates */
        For K = 1 to 4
            A1 = A1 + F (K) * Parray (K,1)
            A2 = A2 + F (K) * Parray (K,2)
        Next K
        Oarray (Count,1) = A1
        Oarray (Count,2) = A2
    Next Count
End of Cubicfit subroutine
```

Figure 8.17   Multiple cubic curves

one another at their start and endpoints. When describing curves with a set of points P1, P2, . . . P8 (and generally, any even number greater than 4), you have to choose additional points between P3 and P4 and between P5 and P6 and so on to indicate where the parts of the curves are to join. If there are N even points, there are N/2 −1 segments of the curve to draw and, hence, the same number of calls to Cubicfit. The first would use points P1, P2, P3 and the intermediate point, P3/P4; the second would use point P3/P4, P4, P5 and the intermediate point, P5/P6; and the third would use points P5/P6, P6, P7 and P8. It can be seen that the bounding lines give a crude indication of the shape of the final curve.

Exercises

8.1 Code the different ways we have given to create the coordinates of a circle. Write a test program to generate a circle of radius 10 centred at (10,10) and use this to compare the time taken by each method. To compare like with like, ensure that the same number of points is generated in each case. You will probably find it easier to time five circles rather than one and this will also allow you to compare the performance of Unitcircle with the rest. Remember to call Unitcircle just once and to multiply the resulting coordinates by 10 and shift to (10,10) in the manner of Table 8.7.

8.2 Put Three-pt-circle into your computer system adding a test for colinearity in the place indicated. Check your programming with the points (12.071,17.071), (13.66, 15) and (10, 1.34): you should arrive at a circle of radius very close to 10 centred at (5,10). What happens if two of the input points are the same? Put in a test to ensure that three separate points are used.

8.3 Using your coding of the subroutine Anglecalc, confirm that the line (5,10) to (13.66, 15) makes an angle of 30 degrees to the horizontal axis. Also show that the line from (5, 10) to (−12.071, 17.071) gives an angle of 135 degrees.

8.4 Using the subroutine Tparcinfo with the points (12.071, 17.071), (13.66, 15) and (10, 1.34), confirm the centre, radius, start and end angles of the arc are (5, 10), 10, 45 degrees and −60 degrees respectively.

8.5 Code the Polyfit subroutine and set it in a test program to check the examples given in the text.

8.6 Using Cubicfit, draw a curve controlled by the four points (0,0), (4,4), (6,5) and (8,0). Do the same with the points (0,0), (4,−4), (6,5) and (8,0). Confirm that the bounding lines joining the control points follow the basic shape of the curve.

8.7 Write a subroutine using more than four control points to make compound curves. This subroutine should call Cubicfit as many times as necessary.

9

2-D Transformations

Having devised a model of the 2-D object we wish to represent, we can then deal with its positioning and orientation in world coordinate space. We need to be able to do this for two reasons:

1 Because our drawings might require the object to move, spin or change in size.
2 Because we may have chosen to describe the object in its simplest position and orientation in order to minimise our own work. It is, after all, very much easier to work out the coordinates of, say, a unit square which is centred about the origin with its sides parallel to the axes, than one which measures 13.46 × 13.46, is tilted over at an angle of 42 degrees and is centred about the point (15.4,−36.276).

In order to achieve correct movement, positioning and orientation, we have to perform some geometric manipulation or transformation of our model. The transformations which enable us to do this are:

1 **Translation**, in order to move the object to its correct position.
2 **2-D rotation**, in order to move the object into its correct orientation.
3 **Scaling**, in order to change the size and possibly the proportions of the object.
4 **Shearing**, in order to change the shape of the object by differentially moving some of its vertices.

Translation, rotation and scaling are common transformations and any graphic system must cope easily with them. Shearing, on the other hand, is rarely needed.

Translation

When we translate a 2-D object we simply add the amount of movement in the X-direction to all the X-coordinates of the model and the amount of movement in the Y-direction to all the Y-coordinates. We can do this directly so that, given a movement in the X-direction of Xmv and a movement in the Y-direction of Ymv, the new coordinates can be calculated from the old by means of the formulae:

$$Xnew = Xold + Xmv$$
$$Ynew = Yold + Ymv$$

Note that it is sufficient to translate only the endpoints of the lines for the whole figure to move to its new position and that if Xmv is negative then we shift to the left. If Ymv is negative then we shift downwards.

2-D rotation

If the point (Xold,Yold) is rotated about the origin by A degrees, the new position has coordinates (Xnew,Ynew) given by:

$$Xnew = Xold * Cos(A) - Yold * Sin (A)$$
$$Ynew = Xold * Sin(A) + Yold * Cos(A)$$

To rotate an object clockwise we use negative values of A and to turn it anticlockwise we use positive angles. In matrix notation this can be written:

$$(Xnew,Ynew) = (Xold,Yold) * \begin{pmatrix} Cos(A) & Sin (A) \\ -Sin (A) & Cos(A) \end{pmatrix}$$

(See Appendix 1 for details of matrix notation and manipulation.)

We can demonstrate that this formulation is true by use, once again, of the sum of the angles formulae and Figure 9.1:

$$
\begin{aligned}
Xnew &= R * Cos(A + Q) \\
&= R * (Cos(A) * Cos(Q) - Sin(A) * Sin(Q)) \\
&= R * Cos(Q) * Cos(A) - R * Sin(Q) * Sin(A) \\
&= Xold * Cos(A) - Yold * Sin(A)
\end{aligned}
$$

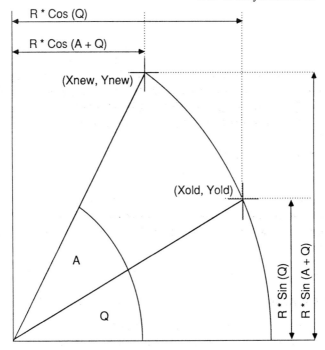

Figure 9.1 Sums of angles formula

Ynew = R * Sin(A + Q)
  = R * (Sin(A) * Cos(Q) + Sin(Q) * Cos(A))
  = R * Cos(Q) * Sin(A) + R * Sin(Q) * Cos(A)
  = Xold * Sin(A) + Yold * Cos(A)

This describes the method for rotating a 2-D object in the two-dimensional X–Y plane. It is, of course, perfectly feasible to rotate a 2-D object in 3-D space but we will deal with this possibility when we look at 3-D rotations.

Scaling

We can scale an object equally in the X- and Y-directions, in which case its size (and, perhaps, its position relative to the origin) changes but its proportions remain the same (Figure 9.2). Alternatively, we

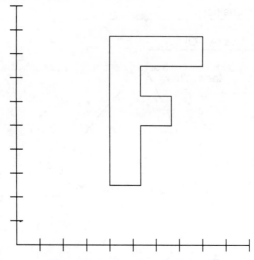

Figure 9.2   Letter F scaled by 1.25

can scale the X- and Y-coordinates by different amounts and this has the effect of changing size, proportions and, possibly, position (Figure 9.3).

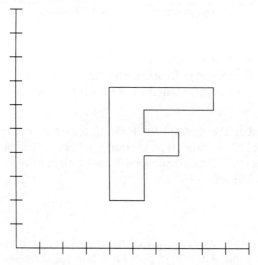

Figure 9.3   Letter F scaled in X-direction only

Scaling is achieved by multiplying each of the X- and Y-coordinates by an appropriate scaling factor. Thus:

Xnew = Xold * Xsc
Ynew = Yold * Ysc

or, in matrix notation:

$$(Xnew, Ynew) = (Xold, Yold) * \begin{pmatrix} Xsc & 0 \\ 0 & Ysc \end{pmatrix}$$

Scaling factors greater than 1 stretch the figure, those between 0 and 1 shrink it. Negative scaling factors produce a variety of reflections the investigation of which is left to the exercises.

Shearing

The shearing transformation has the effect of translating different parts of the object by different amounts so that distortion results (Figure 9.4).

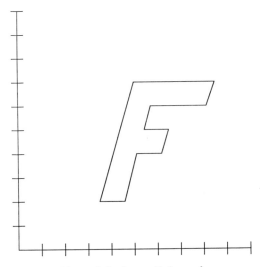

Figure 9.4 Letter F sheared

Shear in the Y-direction is given by:

Xnew = Xold
Ynew = Yold + Xold * Ysh

Shear in the X-direction is given by:

Xnew = Xold + Yold * Xsh
Ynew = Yold

The matrix equivalents of these formulae are:

$$(Xnew, Ynew) = (Xold, Yold) * \begin{pmatrix} 1 & Ysh \\ 0 & 1 \end{pmatrix}$$

$$(Xnew, Ynew) = (Xold, Yold) * \begin{pmatrix} 1 & 0 \\ Xsh & 1 \end{pmatrix}$$

Homogeneous coordinates

We have given the matrix methods of dealing with all the transformations except translation. This is not an oversight but arises from the nature of the coordinate system we have been using so far. Matrix multiplication cannot cope with translation in the normal coordinate system. There is, however, another form of coordinates which is widely used in computer graphics and which makes matrix manipulation more consistent and, perhaps, easier to understand. This is the so-called *homogeneous coordinate system*.

Homogeneous coordinates were originally conceived in order to assist mathematicians in proving theorems about projective geometry – the branch of mathematics concerned with, among other things, perspective. They are used in computer graphics mainly to allow separate matrices for translation, rotation, scaling and (as will be seen), perspective, to be incorporated into one single matrix which can be used to transform coordinates by multiplication only.

Homogeneous coordinates are of a dimension one higher than that of the space they relate to. Thus homogeneous coordinates for 2-D space are of the form (Wx, Wy, W) and, for 3-D space, of the form (Wx, Wy, Wz, W). They are converted back to the required dimension by dividing through by the W-coordinate (it is never equal to zero) and then omitting it from consideration. Thus (Wx,Wy,W) becomes (X,Y) and (Wx,Wy,Wz,W) becomes (X,Y,Z).

As W can take any value other than zero, it can be seen that a point in the homogeneous coordinate system can be represented in an infinity of ways. For example, the point (2,3) in 2-D space can be represented in homogeneous coordinates by (2,3,1) where $W = 1$, (1,1.5,0.5) where $W = 0.5$, (18,27,9) where $W = 9$, and so on. The W coordinate can be thought of as a scaling factor which, for most purposes, is set to 1.

Translation
To translate a point (Xold,Yold) by the amounts Xmv,Ymv we have the matrix:

$$T = \begin{pmatrix} 1 & 0 & 0 \\ 0 & 1 & 0 \\ Xmv & Ymv & 1 \end{pmatrix}$$

We premultiply this by the vector (Xold,Yold,1) giving:

$$(Xnew,Ynew,1) = (Xold,Yold,1) * T$$
$$= (Xold + Xmv, Yold + Ymv, 1)$$

Note that, by use of homogeneous coordinates, we have been able to make a translation (which only involves addition) into a multiplication.

Rotation
For rotation by an angle A we have:

$$R = \begin{pmatrix} C & S & 0 \\ -S & C & 0 \\ 0 & 0 & 1 \end{pmatrix}$$

where $C = Cos (A)$ and $S = Sin (A)$.
Thus,

$$(Xnew,Ynew,1) = (Xold,Yold,1) * R$$
$$= (Xold * C - Yold * S, Xold * S + Yold * C, 1)$$

Scaling

To scale the position of a point by the amounts Xsc,Ysc we use:

$$S = \begin{pmatrix} Xsc & 0 & 0 \\ 0 & Ysc & 0 \\ 0 & 0 & 1 \end{pmatrix}$$

(Xnew,Ynew,1) = (Xold,Yold,1) * S
= (Xold * Xsc, Yold * Ysc, 1)

Inverses

It is important that we have ways of undoing or inverting the effects of matrix transformations. The forms we have given have simple inverses:

1 To invert the translation matrix, use −Xmv,−Ymv,1.
2 To invert the rotation matrices, use the negative of the rotation angle.
3 To invert the scaling matrix, use 1/Xsc,1/Ysc,1.

This simple approach will not work if a matrix has been made into a compound one by multiplying together rotations, scalings and translations – a process known as *concatenation*. In that case, the inverse has to be calculated by standard matrix algebra techniques.

Concatenation

To perform compound moves and rotations, the separate matrices can either be applied consecutively to the coordinate description, or the transformations can be concatenated into a single matrix. This latter approach is likely to be the most efficient if large numbers of points have to be transformed. Thus, to give a rotation in the X–Y plane about a point (Xpt,Ypt,1), we have:

(Xnew,Ynew,1) = (Xold,Yold,1) * T * R * inv(T)

$$\text{where } T = \begin{pmatrix} 1 & 0 & 0 \\ 0 & 1 & 0 \\ -Xpt & -Ypt & 1 \end{pmatrix}$$

$$R = \begin{pmatrix} C & S & 0 \\ -S & C & 0 \\ 0 & 0 & 1 \end{pmatrix}$$

$$\text{inv(T)} = \begin{pmatrix} 1 & 0 & 0 \\ 0 & 1 & 0 \\ \text{Xpt} & \text{Ypt} & 1 \end{pmatrix}$$

What we are doing by applying the matrices is, firstly, to move the object to the origin, then to rotate it about the origin and, finally, to move it back again to its original position. The effect of this is to rotate the object in place about the point (Xpt,Ypt).

In a program we would normally set up a new single matrix, Con, where Con is given by:

Con = T * R * inv(T)

and this would be used instead of the three separate ones. It is left as an exercise for you to show that:

$$\text{Con} = \begin{pmatrix} C & S & 0 \\ -S & C & 0 \\ A & B & 1 \end{pmatrix}$$

where A = −Xpt * C + Ypt * S + Xpt
and   B = −Xpt * S − Ypt * C + Ypt

It has to be noted that, unless the computer system you use is designed to handle matrix manipulation with special efficiency or if, as in APL or some versions of BASIC, matrix handling is part of the language, it is probably computationally faster to use the specific formulae given rather than the matrix versions of them. However, as most textbooks and papers on computer graphics use matrix methods to describe transformations, it is useful to become familiar with the techniques.

Exercises

9.1 Write and test a subroutine to perform translation on a set of N coordinates. The input parameters of the subroutine should be N; the names of the arrays containing the X- and Y-coordinates; Xmv and Ymv, the distances to be moved. It should return Num, the number of pairs of points and Num pairs of X–Y points in an output array.

9.2   Use the subroutine to show that the line from (5,7) to (9,9), when translated −6 units in the X-direction and 3.3 in the Y-direction, becomes a line from (−1,10.3) to (3,12.3).

9.3   Code and test a subroutine to perform rotation on a similar set of points. The angle of rotation, Ang, should replace Xmv and Ymv. Ang should be accepted in degrees (so ensure that you make the necessary conversion to radians in the subroutine if your system requires it). It is important to note that transformation subroutines will be called many times in 2-D graphics programming, so they should be coded as efficiently as you can. In particular, remember to work at the maximum accuracy that your system permits. Do not round off to integers until you actually want to plot the points.

9.4   Use the subroutine to test that the line from (5,7) to (9,9) becomes a line from (0.081,8.6) to (2.21,12.535) when rotated by 35 degrees about the origin. Rotate the original line through −40 degrees. Show that it then runs from (8.33,2.148) to (12.68,1.11).

9.5   We have rotated the line about the origin. For this exercise rotate the line about its endpoint (5,7). To do this remember to move this endpoint to the origin, make the rotation, and then move it back to its original position again. This will mean calling the translation subroutine twice. The line rotated by 35 degrees about (5,7) should have the new coordinates (5,7) and (7.13,10.93). The results for −40 degrees should be (5,7) and (9.35,5.96).

9.6   Write a subroutine using homogeneous coordinates so that Exercise 9.5 can be done with matrix multiplication only. Employ the method outlined in the section on Concatenation.

10

2-D Clipping and Window to Viewport Mapping

The next task we have to perform is to clip the picture to the dimensions of the surface on which we wish it to be displayed. We do this by trimming off any lines which might fall outside the window and then mapping the window onto the display area viewport. Some graphics systems are able to deal with these tasks directly by including commands to allow us to define windows and viewports to which they clip. Such commands might be of the form:

Clip (on)
Window (Wleft,Wright,Wlow,Whigh)
Viewport (Vleft,Vright,Vlow,Vhigh)

These commands map the window onto the viewport in the manner of Figure 10.1 and ensure that only points that lie within the

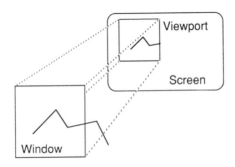

Figure 10.1   Window to viewport mapping with clipping

viewport are displayed. Many systems, especially personal computer systems, do not provide these window/viewport and clipping facilities so we have to write our own subroutines to prevent the undesirable results which might arise if we attempt to draw outside the display area. Three different types of problem could arise unless we take steps to prevent them:

1 The lines will 'wrap around', going out of one edge of the screen and returning on the opposite edge, ruining the picture with extraneous lines.
2 In the case of plotters, the pen can jam against the sides of the display surface, possibly damaging the device in the process.
3 The system may simply fail, thus preventing any further work until it is re-started.

Fortunately, the mathematics of mapping and 2-D clipping are fairly easy, although, in order to perform clipping quickly, the subroutines incorporating the algorithms should really be in machine code.

Clipping

The need for clipping arises if either (or both) of the endpoints of any lines lie outside the window and, hence, should not be seen. There are three cases to consider:

1 When the whole line is invisible.
2 When only part of the line is visible.
3 When the whole line is visible.

If both endpoints are within the window, then the whole of the line is visible. If one end is within the window and the other not, then part of the line is visible. These are quite easy situations to deal with. Rather more difficulties arise when both endpoints lie outside the window. When this happens, either the whole line can be invisible, or only the middle part can be seen. Figure 10.2 illustrates these possibilities.

To deal with all the eventualities, any clipping algorithm must have the following outline form:

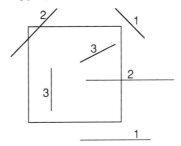

Figure 10.2 Line clipping

Lines of type 1 are wholly invisible.
Lines of type 3 are wholly visible.
Lines of type 2 are partly visible, so their intersections with the clipping boundaries have to be calculated.

Check case of:

1 Line completely invisible.
2 Line partially visible.
3 Line completely visible.

Then, for

Case 1: ignore the line.
Case 2: work out intersection of the line with boundaries of windows and include new line.
Case 3: include complete line.

To cope with Case 2, we need to be able to calculate the point of intersection of two lines: the arbitrary line we are considering and one of the window boundaries. Fortunately, the window boundaries are either horizontal or vertical and this makes the mathematics fairly simple. First of all, though, we must check which case applies. For this, we need a routine which classifies the line by looking at the position of its ends. One such routine is based on the Cohen-Sutherland algorithm (named after two pioneers in computer graphics who first proposed it). In its original form, this uses an ingenious technique of bit-manipulation to work out the cases. Working at the bit-level is useful when you want to write programs in machine code. For more generality, we will use a modified form which makes high-level programming easier.

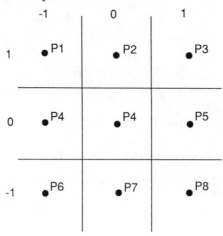

Figure 10.3   Clipping codes

If we consider the window to be lying in the centre of a 3×3 grid which has its squares coded in the manner of Figure 10.3, we can see that any point in the grid can be assigned a unique combination of Xcode and Ycode values according to its position. These combinations can be summarised as in Table 10.1. As can be seen from this table, any line which has both its endpoints within the centre square (and is thus completely visible) has both Xcode and Ycode equal to zero. We can assign these clipping codes and do the necessary

Table 10.1

Point	Xcode	Ycode
P1	-1	1
P2	0	1
P3	1	1
P4	-1	0
P5	0	0
P6	1	0
P7	-1	-1
P8	0	-1
P9	1	-1

Clipcodes

Table 10.2   *Clipcodes* subroutine

```
Subroutine Clipcodes (Xw, Yw; Xcode, Ycode)
Integer Xcode, Ycode
Real Xw, Yw
/* Calculates the Xcode and Ycode of any point (Xw,Yw) given window
details defined globally. Window centre is Xmove, Ymove away from origin
*/
Global Real Xmove, Ymove, Xbound, Ybound
Local Real Xnew, Ynew
    Xnew = Xw − Xmove
    Ynew = Yw − Ymove
    If Abs (Xnew) > Xbound Then
        Xcode = Sgn (Xnew)
    Else
        Xcode = 0
    Endif
    If Abs (Ynew) > Ybound Then
        Ycode = Sgn (Ynew)
    Else
        Ycode = 0
    Endif
End of Clipcodes subroutine
```

Table 10.3   *Clipline* subroutine

```
Subroutine Clipline (X1old, Y1old, X2old, Y2old; X1n, Y1n, X2n, Y2n, Vis)
Integer Vis
Real X1old, Y1old, X2old, Y2old, X1n, Y1n
/* Defines the clipped points (X1n,Y1n) and (X2n,Y2n) given the points
(X1old,Y1old) and (X2old,Y2old) */
Local Real Ratio
/* Find Clipcodes for the end points */
    Call Clipcodes (X1old, Y1old; X1code, Y1code)
    Call Clipcodes (X2old, Y2old; X2code, Y2code)
/* Ignore points which lie in same off-screen region */
    If X1code * X2code = 1 or Y1code * Y2code = 1 Then
        Vis = 0        /* Line not visible */
        X1n = X1old
        Y1n = Y1old
        X2n = X2old
        Y2n = Y2old
    Else
/* Move the line to the centralised window */
```

```
      X1n = X1old - Xmove
      Y1n = Y1old - Ymove
      X2n = X2old - Xmove
      Y2n = Y2old - Ymove
 /* Clip line from point 1 to nearer X-edge */
    If X1code <> 0 Then
      Xtemp = Xbound * X1code
      Ratio = (Xtemp - X1n) / (X2n - X1n)
      Y1n = Y1n + (Y2n - Y1n) * Ratio
      X1n = Xtemp
/* Find Clipcodes for shortened line */
      Call Clipcodes (X1n + Xmove, Y1n + Ymove; X1code, Y1code)
    Endif
/* Clip line from point 1 to nearer Y-edge */
    If Y1code <> 0 Then
      Ytemp = Ybound * Y1code
      Ratio = (Ytemp - Y1n) / (Y2n - Y1n)
      X1n = X1n + (X2n - X1n) * Ratio
      Y1n = Ytemp
    Endif
/* Clip line from point 2 to nearer X-edge */
    If X2code <> 0 Then
      Xtemp = Xbound * X2code
      Ratio = (Xtemp - X1n) / (X2n - X1n)
      Y2n = Y1n + (Y2n - Y1n) * Ratio
      X2n = Xtemp
/* Find Clipcodes for shortened line */
      Call Clipcodes (X2n + Xmove, Y2n + Ymove; X2code, Y2code)
    Endif
/* Clip line from point 2 to nearer Y-edge */
    If Y2code <> 0 Then
      Ytemp = Ybound * Y2code
      Ratio = (Ytemp - Y1n) / (Y2n - Y1n)
      X2n = X1n + (X2n - X1n) * Ratio
      Y2n = Ytemp
    Endif
    Vis = 1          /* some part is visible */
/* Move line back to original position */
    X1n = X1n + Xmove
    Y1n = Y1n + Ymove
    X2n = X2n + Xmove
    Y2n = Y2n + Ymove
    Endif
End of Clipline subroutine
```

clipping of lines by means of two subroutines which we call Clip-codes and Clipline (Tables 10.2 and 10.3).

These work on the assumption that the window is placed centrally about the origin. However, the particular window we want to use might not be central (as in Figure 10.4, for example), so we must calculate the amounts by which our window and lines should be moved. This is done in the Set-window routine shown in Table 10.4.

The dimensions of the viewport are established by the routine Set-wsviewport. It assumes that the maximum and minimum possible sizes for the device have been set earlier in the program. These values are Xvx, Yvx, Xvn, Yvn and are integers. Set-wsviewport is shown in Table 10.5.

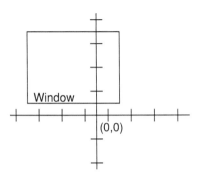

Figure 10.4   Off-centre window

Table 10.4   *Set-window* subroutine

```
Subroutine Set-window (Wxmin, Wxmax, Wymin, Wymax)
Real Wxmin, Wxmax, Wymin, Wymax
/* Sets the global parameters for the window */
Global Real Wleft, Wright, Wlow, Whigh, Xmove, Ymove, Xbound, Ybound
    Wleft  = Wxmin
    Wright = Wxmax
    Wlow   = Wymin
    Whigh  = Wymax
/* Check that the parameters are in the right order */
    If Wleft >= Wright or Wlow >= Whigh Then
        Print 'Window definition is invalid'
        Stop
    Endif
```

```
/* Calculate amounts to move window centre to origin */
    Xmove = (Wright + Wleft) * 0.5
    Ymove = (Whigh + Wlow) * 0.5
/* Determine the new boundaries */
    Xbound = Wright - Xmove
    Ybound = Whigh - Ymove
End of Set-window subroutine
```

Table 10.5 *Set-wsviewport* subroutine

```
Subroutine Set-wsviewport (Vxmin,Vxmax,Vymin,Vymax)
Integer Vxmin, Vxmax, Vymin, Vymax
/* Sets global dimensions for the viewport in device coordinates */
Global Integer Vleft, Vright, Vlow, Vhigh, Xvx, Yvx, Xvn, Yvn
    Vleft  = Vxmin
    Vright = Vxmax
    Vlow   = Vymin
    Vhigh  = Vymax
/* Check that parameters are in right order */
    If Vleft >= Vright or Vlow >= Vhigh Then
        Print 'Viewport definition is invalid'
        Stop
    Endif
/* Check that requested viewport is not bigger than allowable */
    If Vleft < Xvn or Vright > Xvx or Vlow < Yvn or Vhigh > Xvx Then
        Print 'Viewport dimensions are invalid'
        Stop
    Endif
End of Set-wsviewport subroutine
```

Window to viewport mapping

The computation of window/viewport mapping from world to device coordinates for any point (Xw,Yw) is done using the descriptions of Figure 10.5 and the formulae:

$$Xscale = (Vright - Vleft) / (Wright - Wleft)$$
$$Yscale = (Vhigh - Vlow) / (Whigh - Wlow)$$
$$Xv = (Xw - Wleft) * Xscale + Vleft$$
$$Yv = (Yw - Wlow) * Yscale + Vlow$$

These formulae take the point (Xw,Yw) in world coordinates to the point (Xv,Yv) in device coordinates. The Xscale and Yscale

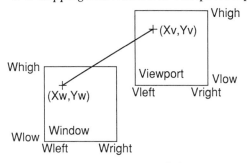

Figure 10.5   Window and viewport

calculations need only be carried out once, directly after the window and viewport dimensions have been set. You should write a subroutine called Makescales to do this. The (Xw,Yw) to (Xv, Yv) calculations need to be done for the endpoints of every line to be displayed. A subroutine called Viewtrans could cater for this.

Sometimes we want a viewport which covers the whole of a display surface; on other occasions, only part of the surface would be needed. For a device with a resolution of 280 × 160, a window of −558 to 558 by −40 to 596, and a viewport covering the whole of the display area (Figure 10.6), our formulae would work as follows:

Vright $= 279$		Wright $=$	558
Vleft $=$	0	Wleft $=$	-558
Vhigh $= 159$		Whigh $=$	596
Vlow $=$	0	Wlow $=$	-40

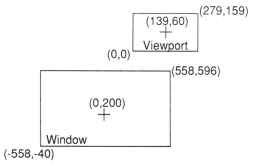

Figure 10.6   Window to viewport mapping

$$\text{Xscale} = 279 / 1116 \qquad = 0.25$$
$$\text{Yscale} = 159 / 636 \qquad = 0.25$$
$$\text{Xv} = (\text{Xw} + 558) * 0.25$$
$$\text{Yv} = (\text{Yw} + 40 \ ) * 0.25$$

The point (0,200) in world coordinates would therefore map to (139.5,60) in device coordinates thus:

$$\text{Xv} = (0 + 558) * 0.25 = 139.5$$
$$\text{Yv} = (200 + 40) * 0.25 = 60.0$$

For many systems it will be necessary to truncate the device coordinates, Xv and Yv, into integers before sending them to the display – otherwise an error condition will be set up. For this reason, we should use (139,60) rather than (139.5,60.0).

For a device with a resolution of 1280×1024, a window of -70 to 90 by 28 to 156, and a viewport covering the top right hand quadrant of the display surface (Figure 10.7), our formulae become:

Vright = 1279	Wright = 90
Vleft = 639	Wleft = −70
Vhigh = 1023	Wxhi = 156
Vlow = 511	Wxlo = 28

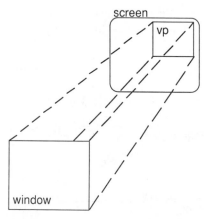

Figure 10.7   Window/viewport mapping

Xscale = (1279 − 639) / (90 + 70)
    = 640 / 160 = 4
Yscale = (1023 − 511) / (156 − 28)
    = 512 / 128 = 4

In this configuration, a point (25,100) in world coordinates would map to (1019,799) in device coordinates, thus:

Xv = (25 + 70) ∗ 4 + 639 = 1019
Yv = (100 − 28) ∗ 4 + 511 = 799

To avoid distortion of our pictures, we have carefully tailored these two examples so that the shape of the window matches that of the viewport – thus making Xscale equal to Yscale. If it is important that distortion does not occur, you should always ensure that the proportions of the viewport and window coincide in any of your drawings. To facilitate this you might consider using only square windows and viewports unless there are special reasons for doing otherwise. The viewport should be the largest square that can be drawn on the display. For displays of horizontal aspect, the sides of the square will thus be equal to the height.

Viewports in normalised device coordinates

When we set our viewport coordinates in the previous examples, we used the actual dimensions of the devices we were drawing to. This is a speedy and satisfactory method if we always intend to draw to the same display but, as pointed out in Chapter 6, it is useful to write programs to allow us to draw to any appropriate device. To facilitate this so-called device independence, normalised device coordinates (NDCs) and normalised transformations are used. In this case, we employ the same method of describing our windows as before, but viewports are set in dimensions ranging from 0 to 1 in both directions regardless of the sizes and shapes of the display surfaces we might use. When we come to display the picture on a new device we merely have to scale it to the proper dimensions.

A new subroutine, Set-viewport, needs to be written to accomplish this. Set-viewport would be like Set-wsviewport but, to test for allowable ranges, we should use Xmin = 0, Xmax = 1, Ymin = 0 and Yvmax = 1. The viewport size message should be changed to 'Viewport is not within the NDC unit square'.

Our previous example would then take the following form:

Set-window (−90,90,28,156)
Set-viewport (0.5,1.0,0.5,1.0)
Makescales
Viewtrans (Xw,Yw;Xv,Yv)

The Makescales and Viewtrans subroutines (which you should have created as exercises) could be as in Tables 10.6 and 10.7. Thus, after passing through the subroutines:

Xscale = 0.003125
Yscale = 0.003906
Xndc　= 0.796875
Yndc　= 0.781246

so that the point (25,100) in world coordinates becomes point (0.796875,0.781246) in NDCs.

Table 10.6　*Makescales* subroutine

Subroutine Makescales
Global Integer Vleft, Vright, Vlow, Vhigh
Global Real Xscale, Yscale, Wright, Wleft, Whigh, Wlow
/* Globally sets Xscale and Yscale from window and viewport parameters.
You should include a check that division by zero will not arise as it will if
Wright = Wleft or Whigh = Wlow */
　　Xscale = (Vright − Vleft) / (Wright − Wleft)
　　Yscale = (Vhigh − Vlow) / (Whigh − Wlow)
End of Makescales subroutine

Table 10.7　*Viewtrans* subroutine

Subroutine Viewtrans (Xcoord, Ycoord; Xndc, Yndc)
Real Xcoord, Ycoord, Xndc, Yndc
/* Converts a point (Xcoord,Ycoord) in world coordinates to a point
(Xndc,Yndc) in NDCs. VNleft and VNlow are also in NDCs */
Global Real Wleft, Wlow, Xscale, Yscale, VNleft, VNlow
　　Xndc = (Xcoord − Wleft) * Xscale + VNleft
　　Yndc = (Ycoord − Wlow) * Yscale + VNlow
End of Viewtrans subroutine

Multiple viewports

Sometimes we want to make drawings built up of a number of windows and viewports on the same display surface in the manner of Figure 10.8. We can do this either by changing the parameters of the Set-window and the Set-viewport or Set-wsviewport subroutines whenever we need to, or by defining a number of windows and viewports at the beginning of our program and calling on these as necessary. In some circumstances (particularly when we are jumping from one viewport to another many times in a program), the latter procedure is preferable and, in order to accomplish this, we should modify our subroutines to let us specify a code number to

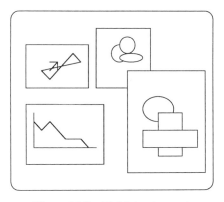

Figure 10.8 Multiple viewports

Table 10.8

```
/* Part of a program with mutiple windows and viewports */
Call Set-window (1,0,100,0,90)        /* window 1 */
Call Set-viewport (1,0,0.5,0,0.5)      /* viewport 1 */
Call Set-window (2,25,75,10,80)        /* window 2 */
Call Set-viewport (2,0.5,1.0,0.5,1.0)  /* viewport 2 */
   Call Makescales (1)
   Call Viewtrans (1)
   Call Makescales (2)
   Call Viewtrans (2)
/* End of program fragment */
```

distinguish between different combinations. The parameter lists and the body of the subroutines should be altered to accept a code number and to keep a record of the different values. A program fragment might then take the form of Table 10.8.

Polygon clipping

Many of the drawings we wish to display will be made up of polygons rather than single lines. When a set of lines making up a polygon such as those in Figure 10.9a are submitted to our clipping routine, the following changes occur:

1   Line P1–P2 is clipped at point PC2 (Figure 10.9b).
2   Line P2–P3 is clipped altogether and rendered invisible (Figure 10.9c).
3   Line P3–P1 is clipped at point PC1 (Figure 10.9d).

What we have left is a pair of lines rather than a polygon. This will not matter if we are drawing only in lines but, if we need to work in polygons (perhaps in order to shade them in), we must be able to

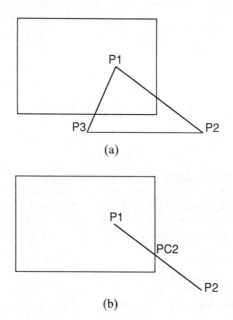

(a)

(b)

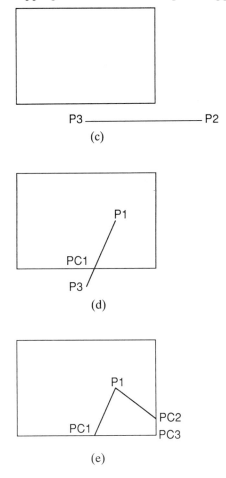

Figure 10.9 Clipping a polygon

treat clipped figures as if they, too, were polygons. This means that the clipped shape of Figure 10.9a should be a polygon of the form shown in Figure 10.9e. Note that, in this case, the new polygon has more sides and vertices than the old one. This will usually be the case. Indeed, as we see from Figure 10.10, sometimes a clipped polygon can have twice the number of sides of an unclipped one.

In order to deal properly with polygons, we need to introduce

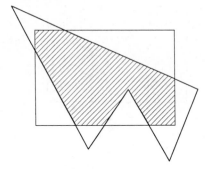

Figure 10.10   Clipped polygons can have twice as many vertices as
unclipped ones

a new subroutine, Clippoly. This differs considerably from our
Cliplines routine and expects to handle a polygon of N vertices. It is
based on a method devised by Sutherland and Hodgman and works
by testing the whole polygon against each of the window boundaries
in turn. Whenever the polygon goes outside one of the boundary
lines (extended indefinitely in each direction) extra vertices are
added and a new polygon is formed in the manner of Figure 10.11.
Because extra vertices are likely to be added at each stage of
boundary testing and as it is impossible to tell ahead of time how
many extra will occur, we must save the new polygons in arrays
which are much larger than the original. This method, then, is not
very efficient in storage. Sutherland and Hodgman's original
method is recursive and uses storage much more sparingly, but,

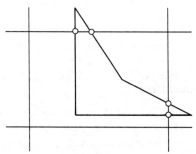

Figure 10.11   Extra vertices added whenever polygon edges cross
clipping lines

because it is not easy to program recursively in some languages, we use a more straightforward version. Unlike Cliplines, Clippoly does not need to move the window to the origin in order to work. This subroutine is given in Table 10.9.

Table 10.9 *Clippoly* subroutine

```
Subroutine Clippoly (N, Inpoly; NN, Outpoly )
Integer N, NN
Real Inpoly, Outpoly
/* Using Edge 1,2,3 or 4 clips a polygon of N vertices described in Inpoly
to a polygon of NN vertices described in Outpoly. Outpoly must have
dimension (2 * N, 2) */
Local Integer I, Count, Edge, J, Vis1, Vis2, Vis3
Local Real Temp, S1, S2, P1, P2, X, Y
/* Define a local Temporary array and copy Inpoly into it */
Dim Temp (2 * N,2)
For I = 1 to N
    Temp(I, 1) = Inpoly(I, 1)
    Temp(I, 2) = Inpoly(I, 2)
Next I
For Edge = 1 to 4  /* For each boundary */
    Count = 1
    S1 = Temp(N, 1) /* point S is the last point */
    S2 = Temp(N, 2)
    For J = 1 to N     /* for each vertex */
        P1 = Temp(J, 1) /* point P is next point */
        P2 = Temp(J, 2)
        Call Visible(Edge, P1, P2; Vis1)
        If (Vis1 = 1) Then  /* point P is visible */
            Call Visible(Edge, S1, S2; Vis2)
            If (Vis2 = 1) Then  /* point S is visible */
                Outpoly(Count, 1) = P1
                Outpoly(Count, 2) = P2
                Count = Count + 1
            Else   /* point S is invisible */
                Call Intersect(Edge, S1, S2, P1, P2; X, Y)
                Outpoly(Count, 1) = X
                Outpoly(Count, 2) = Y
                Count = Count + 1
                Outpoly(Count, 1) = P1
                Outpoly(Count, 2) = P2
                Count = Count + 1
            Endif
```

```
        Else   /* point P is invisible */
           Call Visible(Edge, S1, S2; Vis3)
           If (Vis3 = 1) Then
              Call Intersect(Edge, S1, S2, P1, P2; X, Y)
              Outpoly(Count, 1) = X
              Outpoly(Count, 2) = Y
              Count = Count + 1
           Endif
        Endif
    /* Move to next point */
           S1 = P1
           S2 = P2
        Next J
        NN = Count - 1
        N = NN
        /* Assign temporary array with new polygon */
        For I = 1 to NN
           Temp(I, 1) = Outpoly(I, 1)
           Temp(I, 2) = Outpoly(I, 2)
        Next I
     Next Edge
     End of Clippoly subroutine
```

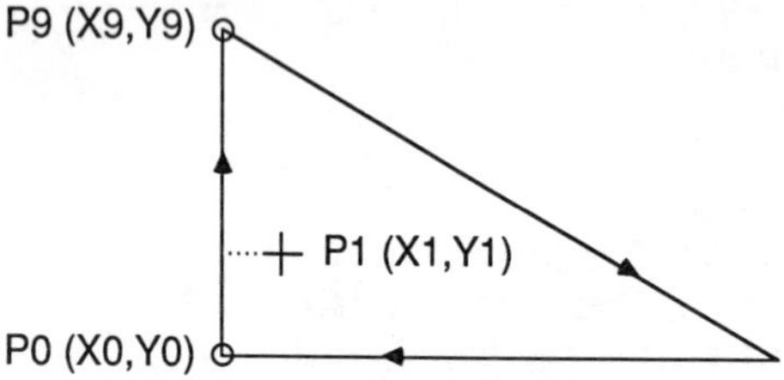

Figure 10.12   P1 is inside because it is always to the right of the lines
(described clockwise).

Clippoly makes use of two other subroutines: Intersect, which determines the point at which a line intersects an exended boundary, and Visible, which decides if a point is inside a boundary. 'Inside' in this context means that a point P1 (X1,Y1) is to the right hand side of a line described from point P0 (X0,Y0) to P9 (X9,Y9) as in Figure 10.12. This happens to be the case if V1 given by the following formula is positive:

$$V1 = (X9 - X0) * (Y9 - Y1) - (Y9 - Y0) * (X9 - X1)$$

Intersect and Visible are listed as Tables 10.10 and 10.11.

Table 10.10 *Intersect* subroutine

```
Subroutine Intersect (Edge, X1, Y1, X2, Y2; X,  Y )
Integer Edge
Real X1,X2,X,Y1,Y2,Y
/* Determines the point (X, Y) at which the line from (X1,Y1) to (X2,Y2)
cuts edge */
Global Real Whigh, Wright, Wlow, Wleft
Local Real R
Case Edge of
   1 :  R = (Whigh - Y1) / (Y2 - Y1)
        X = X1 + (X2 - X1) * R
        Y = Whigh
   2 :  R = (Wright - X1) / (X2 - X1)
        Y = Y1 + (Y2 - Y1) * R
        X = Wright
   3 :  R = (Wlow - Y1) / (Y2 - Y1)
        X = X1 + (X2 - X1) * R
        Y = Wlow
   4 :  R = (Wleft - X1) / (X2 - X1)
        Y = Y1 + (Y2 - Y1) * R
        X= Wleft
Endcase
End of Intersect subroutine
```

Table 10.11 *Visible* subroutine

```
Subroutine Visible (Edge, X1, Y1;  V)
Integer Edge, V
Real X1, Y1
/* Sets V = 1 if point (X1,Y1) is to the visible side of Edge 1,2,3, or 4 */
Global Real Wright, Wleft, Wlow, Whigh
Local Real V1
Case Edge of
   1 :  V1 = (Wright - Wleft) * (Whigh - Y1)
   2 :  V1 = - (Wlow - Whigh) * (Wright - X1)
   3 :  V1 = (Wleft - Wright) * (Wlow - Y1)
   4 :  V1 = - (Whigh - Wlow) * (Wleft - X1)
Endcase
If (V1 <= 0) Then
   V = 0
```

Else
  V = 1
Endif
End of Visible subroutine

Exercises

10.1 If you tackled Exercise 2.4 you will know how your system deals with instructions to draw outside the display area. It may be that the computer does the clipping itself and has its own versions of window and viewport subroutines. If this is the case, try out various window/ viewport combinations to familiarise yourself with the effects. In particular, try setting very large windows, say ›32 000 units wide. Can the system still cope?

10.2 If your system performs correct clipping of screen drawings, check that it also handles clipping on external devices such as plotters. Two possibilities arise:

   1 The clipping is done in the computer and only the clipped information is sent down to the device.
   2 The external device itself can deal with clipping.

   If a device of the second type is connected to the computer by a slow serial line and you are trying to make drawings which have a great deal of clipped information, you may find it better to program your own clipping in order to minimise the amount of 'invisible' data that is sent down the line. Essentially, it is a matter of trading off computation time against communication time. Either program the subroutines given in this chapter and test the differences directly or perform some back-of-envelope calculations to see what savings, if any, might result.

10.3 Code the subroutines given and use these to check the examples given in the text. Try positioning the viewport at different points on the display space.

10.4 Use the coordinates of the letter 'F' given in Chapter 7 in order to examine the way in which different window/viewport settings change shape and proportion.

10.5 The Makescales subroutine as given in Table 10.6 will fail and bring about a system error condition if it is called with either Wright = Wleft or Whigh = Wlow. Why is this? Put a test into the subroutine to guard against the possibility.

10.6 Work out a method to allow you to retain a given aspect ratio between the window and the viewport so that proportion is maintained.

10.7   Try out your subroutines with multiple windows and viewports on the same display surface. Include both overlapping and non-overlapping viewports.

10.8   After coding the various subroutines to perform polygon clipping, check the results with a set of test shapes. Make sure you include polygons which totally surround the window as well as those which are completely inside. If you have any skill with machine coding try writing the subroutines in this form in order to speed up performance.

10.9   Write and test a Set-viewport routine to work with the NDC square as outlined at the beginning of the chapter. Try out different combinations of window, NDC viewport and device viewports. List out the advantages and disadvantages of having this additional step in the drawing process.

11

Display

After we have modelled, transformed and clipped our 2-D objects, we are ready to display them. To do this, we need to make use of the drawing instructions introduced in Chapter 2. The actual appearance of our drawings will depend on the output devices and the software available to us, but given the right facilities, we can draw:

1 In line or in tone.
2 In monochrome or colour.
3 In 'staircased' or 'unstaircased' lines and so on.

In addition, we have the options of displaying our drawings in parts or as a whole, interactively or non-interactively, as single pictures or as a series which make up an animated sequence.

Line drawing

Some display devices, plotters and DVSTs for example, can only be used conveniently for line drawings. On such devices, we can display pictures built up of separate lines with a simple routine like Drawline which uses the graphics primitives MOVE and DRAW (Table 11.1).

Each of the N lines to make up a drawing can then be put through a program fragment as in Table 11.2. This program fragment would deal either with sets of disconnected lines (like grids) or with connected lines (like polygons). However, each call to Drawline

Table 11.1 *Drawline* subroutine

```
Subroutine Drawline (Xstart, Ystart, Xend, Yend)
Integer Xstart, Ystart, Xend, Yend
/* Draws single line from (Xstart,Ystart) to (Xend,Yend). Both points are
expressed in device coordinates */
    MOVE (Xstart, Ystart)
    DRAW (Xend, Yend)
End of Drawline subroutine
```

Table 11.2

```
/* Program fragment to draw N separate lines */
    Set-window (Wxmin, Wxmax, Wymin, Wymax)
    Set-wsviewport (Vxmin, Vxmax, Vymin, Vymax)
    Makescales  /* calculate Xscale and Yscale */
    For J = 1 to N
      Read X1,Y1,X2,Y2
/* There may be some transformations here */
      Call Clipline (X1, Y1, X2, Y2; X1new, Y1new, X2new, Y2new, Vis)
      If Vis = 1 Then   /* Convert world to device coordinates */
        Call Viewtrans (X1new, Y1new; X1v, Y1v)
        Call Viewtrans (X2new, Y2new; X2v, Y2v)
        Call Drawline (X1v, Y1v, X2v, Y2v)
      Endif
    Next J
/* End of program fragment */
```

Table 11.3 *Polyline* subroutine

```
Subroutine Polyline (N, Xarray, Yarray)
Integer N, Xarray, Yarray
/* Draws a continuous line defined by N points. Often Point N is the same
as Point 1. Will draw a single line if N = 2 */
Local Integer J
    MOVE (Xarray(1), Yarray(1)) /* move to the 1st point */
/* Draw to each of the other points */
    For J = 2 to N
      DRAW (Xarray(J), Yarray(J))
    Next J
End of Polyline subroutine
```

involves both a MOVE and a DRAW statement. This is unnecessary if the end of one line is the beginning of the next as it is in a polygon. It is likely that most of our drawings will be made up of polygons of some form, so we need a subroutine to deal with continuous lines. If we assume that the coordinates of the endpoints of these lines are held in two arrays, Xarray and Yarray each of N elements, we can create a subroutine like Polyline shown in Table 11.3.

When we want to make up our drawing out of polygons, a program fragment like that in Table 11.4 would be needed.

Table 11.4

```
/* Program fragment to deal with polygons */
    Call Set-window (Wxmin, Wxmax, Wymin, Wymax)
    Call Set-wsviewport (Vxmin, Vxmax, Vymin, Vymax)
    Call Makescales         /* calculate Xscale and Yscale */
    For Polygon = 1 to Maxpol
      Read N
      For J = 1 to N
        Read Xarray(J), Yarray(J)
      Next J
/* There may be some transformations here */
    Call Clippoly (N, Xarray, Yarray; Newn, Xout,Yout)
/* Convert world to device coordinates here */
    Call Polyline (Newn, Xout,Yout) /* draw polyline */
    Next polygon
/* End of program fragment */
```

Drawing in tone

Line drawings are attractive and useful ways of conveying graphical information. It often happens, though, that we need to shade in areas in order to give emphasis or to improve the appearance of our drawings. For line devices, like plotters or DVSTs, we have to achieve this effect by hatching in the areas with regularly spaced lines as in Figure 11.1. With raster devices, on the other hand, we can completely fill an area by illuminating all its pixels.

Given a polygon described by two arrays Pxarray (N) and Pyarray (N), a suitable procedure for hatching is given by Hatch (Table 11.5), which works in device coordinates. Some languages do not have the Min and Max functions called in this routine. We can simulate them by:

$$\text{Min}(X, Y) = \text{Abs}(X <= Y) * X + \text{Abs}(X > Y) * Y$$
$$\text{Max}(X, Y) = \text{Abs}(X >= Y) * X + \text{Abs}(X < Y) * Y$$

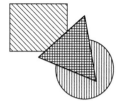

Figure 11.1   Hatching with regularly spaced lines

Table 11.5   *Hatch* subroutine

```
Subroutine Hatch (N, PA, A, D)
Integer N, PA, D
Real A
/* Shades in a closed polygon, PA, of dimension (N, 2) with lines set at
angle A degrees, D device units apart. As this is a display routine, it works
in device coordinates directly on the drawing. The hatching lines are not
stored */
Local Integer JJ, J, K
Local Real P1, Co, L, S, Si, W, W1, W2, X, X1, Y2
   Dim W(N, 2), X(N), P1(2)
   S = 100000
   L = -100000
   A = A * 3.14159/180    /* convert to radians */
   Si = Sin (A)
   Co = Cos (A)
   For JJ = 1 to N        /* rotate polygon through -A */
      W(JJ, 1) = PA(JJ, 1) * Co + PA(JJ, 2) * Si
      W(JJ, 2) = PA(JJ, 2) * Co - PA(JJ, 1) * Si
      S = Min (S, W(JJ, 2))
      L = Max (L, W(JJ, 2))
   Next JJ
   Y2 = S + 0.5 * D
   While Y2 < = L Do
      K = 0
      For JJ = 2 to N
         W1 = Min (W(I-1,2), W(JJ,2))
         If Y2 > = W1 Then
            W2 = Max (W(I-1,2), W(JJ,2))
            If Y2 < W2 Then
               X1 = (W(I-1,2) - Y2) * (W(I-1,1) - W(JJ,1))
               X1= W(I-1,1) - X1 / (W(I-1,2) - W(JJ,2))
               K = K + 1
```

```
            For J = K to 1 Step - 1
                If J = 1 Then
                    X(J) = X1
                Else
                    If X(J-1) => X1 Then
                        X(J) = X1
                        J = 1
                Else
                    X(J) = X (J - 1)
                Endif
                            Endif
                        Next J
                    Endif
                Endif
            Next JJ
            For JJ = 1 to K
                P1(1) = X(JJ) * Co - Y2 * Si    /* rotate back */
                P1(2) = X(JJ) * Si + Y2 * Co
                If 2 * Int (0.5 * JJ) - JJ > - 0.1 Then
                    DRAW (P1(1), P1(2))     /* if JJ odd */
                Else
                    MOVE (P1(1), P1(2))     /* if JJ even */
                Endif
            Next JJ
            Y2 = Y2 + D     /* do next line */
        Endwhile
    End of Hatch subroutine
```

(The absolute values are needed because some systems return -1 for TRUE and 0 for FALSE. If yours returns 1 for TRUE and 0 for FALSE, Abs can be omitted.)

If the display requires it, P1 should be rounded to integers in the last part of the routine. For raster devices, the whole polygon can be filled by means of this subroutine if we set the hatching lines horizontal and draw them at each raster line. Because we have to compute the intersections of each of the closely packed hatching lines with the boundaries of the polygon, this is likely to be a fairly slow process using the subroutine as it stands. It can be speeded up by exploiting the fact that our lines are horizontal and thus have a fairly simple intersection calculation which does not require us to rotate the polygon. We can therefore omit the rotate parts of the subroutine if we intend to use this method.

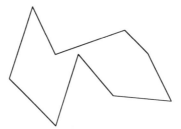

Figure 11.2a   Arbitrary object

Alternatively, in most raster systems we can enquire by program whether any particular pixel is illuminated or not and thus detect the edges of polygons in quite a simple manner. We do this by noting that, as we travel along a raster line and encounter an already illuminated pixel, we are changing from outside the polygon to inside or vice versa. Thus, starting inside a polygon on a particular raster line, we can begin illuminating each pixel right and left until we encounter one which is already illuminated, when we know that we should stop. We then go on to the raster lines above and below and repeat the procedure until the whole is completed.

This simple method will properly deal with convex polygons such as triangles, rectangles and circles, but will not work on a more complicated shape such as that in Figure 11.2a. With such shapes, a particular raster line might cross and recross the boundary a number of times. We can take care of this eventuality by working out the maximum and minimum values of X and Y for the shape and assuming it to lie in a rectangle of these dimensions (less one pixel on each edge) as in Figure 11.2b. We can then continue on any given

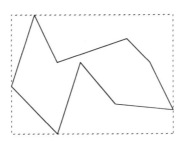

Figure 11.2b   Arbitrary object surrounded by bounding rectangle

raster line switching on the pixels while we are inside the polygon until we reach the boundaries of the surround rectangle when we know that no more edges will be encountered. These methods, of course, require the boundaries of the polygon to be drawn first and will not work if there is even a single pixel gap in the lines. The second method will also interfere with any other parts of the drawing which the bounding rectangle overlaps unless we have a way of determining which already illuminated pixels belong to our particular polygon (as we usually can if they are in a different colour).

Because polygon raster fill is such an important need, a large number of algorithms for doing it efficiently have been published. They fall basically into two forms: Polygon-fill, where just the boundaries of the polygon together with the colour of the fill have to be specified; and Seed-fill, where, in addition, it is necessary to specify a point within the polygon from which the filling spreads. The latter method is usual for paint systems since the seed pixel can be easily pointed to. For high speed, fill algorithms should ideally be programmed in machine code. Many manufacturers now incorporate automatic polygon fill procedures into the firmware of their raster devices and this trend is likely to continue.

Drawing in colour

Most graphics systems using video raster technology let us make drawings in a variety of colours. Home computers often limit the number available to 8 or 16 which are preset by the manufacturers and cannot be altered by the user. In these limited systems, the colours are usually named, or more often numbered, and the choice is made through the use of commands such as COLOUR = RED; HCOLOR = 5; COLOR 3,2; or similar. Many professional systems and even some personal machines, on the other hand, provide a much wider selection which can be tailored to suit particular needs. These systems often allow us to define colours by specifying the percentages of red, green and blue light which make them up. Thus we might issue an instruction like Setcolour (15, 0.7, 0.3, 0) to define colour 15 as a mixture of 70 per cent red and 30 per cent green.

When we set colours by specifying the amounts of red, green and blue in their composition, we are using what is called the RGB colour model. The RGB model can be thought of as a 3-D coordinate system with the primary colour values running from 0 to 1 on the axes and all possible colours lying within a unit cube in the manner of Figure 11.3. The origin (0,0,0) indicates black because zero amounts of each primary are defined and the point (1,1,1) indicates white because full amounts of the three primaries are called for. Anywhere on the diagonal from the origin to point (1,1,1) indicates a shade of grey.

Because we are dealing with the light emitted from glowing phosphors (which themselves have colour limitations), raster systems cannot show all the colours that we can actually see in nature and the colour cube merely indicates the range of colours that a particular system can produce. It should also be noted that, although we may be allowed to specify amounts of primaries in a continuous range from 0 to 1, the digital nature of the controls on the colour guns means that changes actually occur in steps: the finer the steps, the more colours being available to us. To emphasise this fact, some systems require the RGB values to be specified in integers in the range 0 to 255 or 0 to 4095 and so on.

It is not easy for us to work out the correct combinations of red, green and blue needed to produce a particular colour that we have in mind. Some hints can be given to assist:

1   A point along one of the axes produces a shade of a primary, and the closer the point is to the origin, the darker the shade.
2   Points lying in the planes formed by two axes are mixtures of two primaries: mixtures of red and green tend towards yellowish

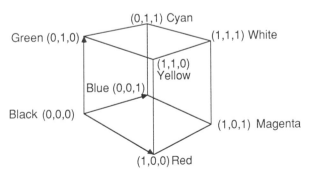

Figure 11.3   The RGB cube

colours, red and blue towards purplish colours, blue and green towards colours which we usually term greenish blues or cyans.

3   Mixtures of three primaries tend towards grey tinged with the colour of the predominant primary. If equal amounts of the three occur, a neutral grey results.
4   Colours sitting on the outer faces of the cube furthest away from the origin are what we usually call tints, that is, they contain a percentage of white.

Some systems have alternative methods of colour specification. One of these derives from the HLS (hue, lightness and saturation) model and some people find this a more satisfactory concept. It has been known since the nineteenth century that we are sensitive to three different components in colour. These are:

1   *Hue*, which is the dominant wavelength of the light and the component which gives the colour its name – red, green, violet and so on. Light whose dominant wavelength is in the region of, say, 578 nm would be called yellow, and 630 nm, red.
2   *Intensity, lightness or brightness* (we tend to use these words as synonyms even though they mean slightly different things). This is the luminous power of the light reaching the eye.
3   *Saturation*, which is the degree to which the hue appears undiluted by white. A colour which seems to have no white in it is said to be saturated. The saturation of a colour is most closely related to the number of wavelengths contributing to it: the fewer the number, the more saturated the colour.

The HLS model attempts to reflect these factors by allowing us to specify separately each of the components which influence our perception of a colour. The HLS model can be visualised as a double cone as illustrated in Figure 11.4. The various hues are arranged around the circles which make the horizontal slices of the cones. In some systems, the hue is specified by its angular measure (in degrees from 0 to 360) often with blue at 0 degrees, red at 120 and green at 240. In other systems, the scale runs from 0 to 1 with blue at 0, red at 0.333 and green at 0.666. The complement of any hue is diametrically opposite it on the circle.

Saturation is indicated by a scale on the radius of any of the hue circles with full saturation (of value 1) being on the circumference.

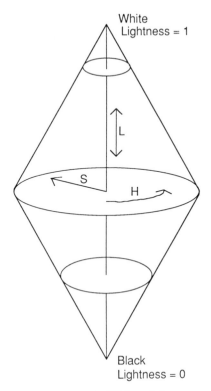

Figure 11.4 HLS model

The axis of lightness runs through the points of the cones from bottom to top. Black has lightness, 0, and white has lightness, 1. Using this system, we might specify a light pink by H = 120, L = 0.7 and S = 0.9.

Whichever method we use for specifying colours (and there are others), it is likely that the system itself uses the colour table technique outlined in Chapter 4 to house the permitted RGB values to be displayed.

Staircased and unstaircased lines

In raster displays, angled lines have a jagged appearance which comes about because they are made up as a series of individual dots

Figure 11.5   A pixel line of slope 5/7 drawn using Bresenham's algorithm

each of which can be thought of as a small 'sample' of the real line. In drawing lines, most raster systems use an algorithm which was devised in the early days of computer graphics and known as Bresenham's algorithm, after its inventor, Jack Bresenham. This ingeniously uses only integer arithmetic (which make it easy to implement in machine code) to ensure that the sample dots are placed as close to their true line as is possible. Figure 11.5 shows a detail of such a line where the slope is 5/7.

A way of eliminating the staircased appearance is to use dots which are so tiny and so close together that the eye cannot separate them from the true line. This would mean using video monitors having about 4000 lines rather than the 500 to 1000 lines that are currently used. However, no one makes such monitors and, if they did, the data rates they would require would present other difficulties. The way in which the problem is tackled is to draw the lines not as single dots of one brightness but as groups of dots of graded brightnesses or grey levels. The effect of this is to produce slightly thicker, fuzzier lines which, at normal viewing distances, we perceive as sharp, straight lines. This technique is known as *anti-aliasing*. A minimum of 16 levels of grey running from white to black (or colours from maximum to minimum lightness) are needed for effective anti-aliasing.

If we look at Figure 11.6, we can see that a line of one pixel width occupies different percentages of each pixel square as it passes across the grid of pixels. It has been found that we can produce lines in which the jaggedness is hidden if the brightness of each pixel is set proportional to the area occupied by the line. Figure 11.7 shows the

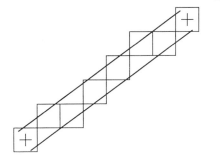

Figure 11.6 A straight line occupies different percentages of each pixel

percentages required by the line of slope 5/7. However, to calculate the percentages is a relatively slow task, so many techniques and shortcuts – including modifications of Bresenham's algorithm – have been suggested to minimise the process. Some new display devices have anti-aliasing methods built in to their hardware and this will become more and more prevalent as time goes on. Figure

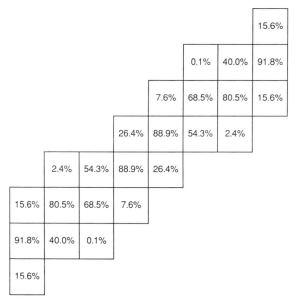

Figure 11.7 Percentage area of line passing through pixels (note the high degree of symmetry)

Table 11.6   *Doros* subroutine

```
Subroutine Doros (Xc, Yc, R)
Real Xc, Yc, R
/* Draws the closest integer approximation to a circle of Radius, R,
centred at (Xc,Yc). The procedure computes and plots the correct points
octant by octant */
Local Integer X, X0, Y, Y0, S, Oct, J
   X0 = Int (Xc + 0.5)        /* Round parameters to nearest integers */
   Y0 = Int (Yc + 0.5)
   S  = Int (R + 0.5)
   X = R                      /* Assign initial values */
   Y = 0
   For Oct = 1 to 8
      If Oct = Int (Oct / 2) * 2 Then         /* Oct is even */
         S = S + 2 * X
         While Y >= 0 Do
            S = S - 2 * Y + 1
            Y = Y - 1
            If S < 0 Then
               S = S + 2 * X + 2
               X = X + 1
            Endif
            If X <> Y Then             /* point is off diagonals */
               Call Point(Oct, X0, Y0, X, Y)
            Endif
         Endwhile
      Else                          /* Oct is odd */
         S = S - 2 * X
         While Y <= X Do
            Call Point (Oct, X0, Y0, X, Y)
            S = S + 2 * Y + 1
            Y = Y + 1
            If S >= 0 Then
               S = S - 2 * X + 2
               X = X - 1
            Endif
         Endwhile
      Endif
   Next Oct
End of Doros subroutine
```

11.8 shows a detail of a line after it has been treated to grey-scale anti-aliasing.

Figure 11.8 Detail of a line treated to grey-scale anti-aliasing (with three grey levels)

Because circles on raster displays are particularly affected by jaggedness, those systems that can draw circles on command tend to use versions of Bresenham's algorithm rather than the many-sided polygon approach we introduced in Chapter 8. One circle-drawing subroutine is typical of this type. It is by a Polish computer scientist, Professor Doros, and creates the circle in eight separate octants. It uses device coordinates and, whilst it does not anti-alias the circle, it does give the best integer fit to it (Table 11.6). Subroutine Doros makes use of Point which, in turn, makes use of Drawline to plot a point (Table 11.7).

Table 11.7 *Point* subroutine

```
Subroutine Point (Oct, X0, Y0, X, Y)
Integer Oct, X0, Y0, X, Y
/* Called from subroutine Doros to plot a point by drawing a line starting
and ending at the same point. If your system has a point plotting primitive,
use this instead */
```

Case of Oct:
    1: **Call** Drawline (X0 + X, Y0 + Y, X0 + X, Y0 + Y)
    2: **Call** Drawline (X0 + Y, Y0 + X, X0 + Y, Y0 + X)
    3: **Call** Drawline (X0 − Y, Y0 + X, X0 − Y, Y0 + X)
    4: **Call** Drawline (X0 − X, Y0 + Y, X0 − X, Y0 + Y)
    5: **Call** Drawline (X0 − X, Y0 − Y, X0 − X, Y0 − Y)
    6: **Call** Drawline (X0 − Y, Y0 − X, X0 − Y, Y0 − X)
    7: **Call** Drawline (X0 + Y, Y0 − X, X0 + Y, Y0 − X)
    8: **Call** Drawline (X0 + X, Y0 − Y, X0 + X, Y0 − Y)
End of Point subroutine

Segments and data structures

Up to now we have used separate arrays to describe the items we wished to draw. Sometimes a single array has been sufficient to deal with an object: sometimes multiple arrays were needed. If we simply want to show objects on a drawing, we can perform transformations on these arrays, clip and display them one after another until the drawing is complete. We can summarise this procedure thus:

    Display Procedure 1
    While there is data do the following:
        Read the number, N, of coordinate points to be expected;
        Read N pairs of coordinates into an array;
        Transform this array as necessary;
        Clip any lines which fall outside the display area and form polylines of the remainder;
        Display these polylines.

In systems with small memories and no disc storage, this is probably the best we can do. To accommodate the description data we only need two or three arrays current at any one time and we can re-use these again and again in order to make drawings of considerable complexity. However, we cannot interact with drawings displayed by this technique. Although we could build up the description interactively, the computer has no knowledge of the structure of a drawing made by this method, so we cannot edit it without changing the underlying data and rerunning the program. To do more than this requires a more comprehensive data structure than we have yet proposed.

In addition, there are a number of reasons why we might want to create and display our drawings in logical sections, each of which represents something complete in its own right. Architect's drawings, for example, might consist of a grid of 1 m squares to indicate sizes; lines showing the outside and inside walls; rectangles and other shapes indicating furniture and so on (Figure 11.9). Sometimes, it might be necessary for all these elements to be shown; on other occasions, only the walls and grid but no furniture, or just the walls themselves, might be more appropriate. Alternatively, in an animation, we might want to keep a background unaltered but move and rotate a foreground object.

These processes of selective display are made easier if we describe our objects as *segments* – parts which can be treated as separate identifiable entities. The idea is that segments can be made visible or invisible, transformed, renamed or deleted without interfering with other parts of the drawing. (The extent to which this idea is realised depends on the characteristics of our display devices. In DVSTs or plotters, for example, we can only add segments to an already displayed drawing. If we wish to make deletions or changes in

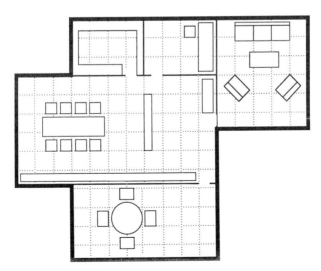

Figure 11.9 Architect's drawing

positions or orientations, it is necessary to redraw the whole picture. Even in raster devices, the selective deletion of parts of a picture often leaves small pixel-sized 'holes' in the drawing where deleted lines cross visible ones.)

To assist in the interactive manipulation of segments, we must be able to identify them by some unique name, and apply separate transformations and attributes to each one. Thus, for instance, we might have Seg1 rotated 30 degrees clockwise and drawn in red solid line; Seg2 made invisible; Seg3 translated to point $(100, -20)$ and drawn in blue dotted line; and so on. With segmented drawings our procedure is this:

Display Procedure 2

For each segment do the following:
   If the segment is to be visible then
   Do Display procedure 1
   Else
   Continue

For Display Procedure 2 to work, we need a data structure to hold details of the points, lines, faces, attributes and transformations in a form which is easy to handle and store.

A simple graphics data structure

Different forms of data structure capable of dealing with segmentation and interaction are possible but we will describe a simple one based on the sorts of arrays we have used so far. The structure is suitable for most systems and languages and requires disc storage. Some languages, such as Pascal and C, permit more complex and powerful arrangements but our structure can be easily modified to take advantage of these facilities.

For each segment, we need a list of the world coordinates of its points together with a list of the point numbers that are to be joined by lines. This latter list is arranged so that the points describe the boundaries of each face. For example, Segment 3 might consist of the letter 'F' surrounded by a box as in Figure 11.10. There are fourteen points in this segment – ten for F and four for the box. The coordinates of these are:

(3,2), (3,7), (6,7), (6,6), (4,6)
(4,5), (5,5), (5,4), (4,4), (4,2)
(2,1), (2,8), (7,8), (7,1)

The line list is:

```
11  /* number of points for F */
1, 2, 3, 4, 5, 6, 7, 8, 9, 10, 1

5   /* number of points for box */
11, 12, 13, 14, 11
```

Figure 11.11 illustrates these lists which will be put onto the disc in named files, one for the points and one for the lines. In addition, we need a *segment table*: an array which keeps a record of the segments and tells the system about their details. The array consists of N rows, one for each segment and M columns, one for each item of information.

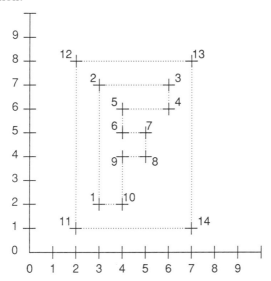

Figure 11.10 Coordinates of letter F and box

For the simplest system, we need five columns arranged as in Figure 11.12. The first column entry holds the number of coordinate points in the segment; the second holds the number of entries in the line list; the third indicates the visibility; the fourth tells us about the

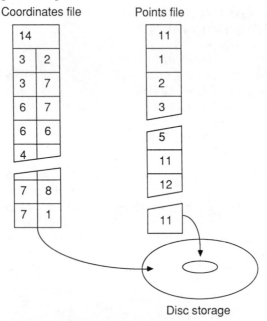

Figure 11.11   Files for drawing Figure 11.10

attributes (such as line style); the fifth says which transformation is to apply to the segment. To access details of a segment – say Segment 3 – we look at row 3 of the table and find that, in this instance, we must expect 14 coordinate points and 18 entries in the line list. As the visibility flag is set to 1, we open arrays to accommodate these data and read them from the disc. We can then

	Points	Lines	Vis	Attr	Trans
	20	22	1	1	1
	4	5	1	1	1
3 →	14	18	1	3	1
	12	12	0	2	2

Figure 11.12   Possible segment table

apply the appropriate transformation to the points and display the lines with the specified attributes.

The points and lines data are held separately in disc files whose names are derived from the generic name of the job and the segment we are dealing with – say, HOUSEPT1, HOUSEPT2 and so on for points and HOUSELN1, HOUSELN2 and so on for the lines. Your disc operating system manual will tell you the form these names can take. Our system has a routine called Makename which takes the generic names and concatenates them with the segment number to produce a single unique identifier.

Associated with the segment table are three global variables: Freeseg, which is the next unused segment number; Currentseg, which is the number of the current segment if it is in use and 0 otherwise; and Maxseg, which is the maximum number of segments we will allow.

To help add, delete and change segments in a simple and ordered way, we need some subroutines. The first of these is Create-segment (Table 11.8).

Table 11.8 *Create-segment* subroutine

```
Subroutine Create-segment (Num)
/* Opens a segment called Num. Puts the system in a state ready to
receive segment information by checking that all is well, setting default
options and opening disc files */
  If Currentseg > Num Then  /* already open? */
    Print 'Segment is already open'
    Stop
  Endif
  If Num < 0 or Num > Maxseg Then  /* any room? */
    Print 'No more room for segments'
    Stop
  Endif
  If Num < Freeseg Then  /* already created? */
    Print 'You already have a segment of this name'
    Stop
  Endif
  /* Apparently OK to continue */
  Freeseg = Freeseg + 1
  Currentseg = Num
  For J = 1 to 5  /* set default values */
    Segtable(Num,J) = 0
```

```
        Next J
        Segtable(Num,3) = 1   /* make visible */
        Call Discop ('open', Num)  /* open disc files */
        End of Create-segment subroutine
```

Segtable should be declared at the beginning of the calling program to Dimension (Maxseg,5). Discop is a subroutine to operate on disc files. Its details depend very much on the computer you use but would take a form similar to Table 11.9.

Table 11.9 *Discop* subroutine

```
Subroutine Discop (Opstring, Num)
/* Opens or closes disc files and sets up their names */
    Call Makename (Pname, Num; Ptfile)  /* for points */
    Call Makename (Lname, Num; Lnfile)  /* for lines */
    If Opstring = 'open' Then   /* open files */
      Open Ptfile for Append as #1
      Open Lnfile for Append as #2
    Else
      If Opstring = 'close' Then  /* close files */
        Close
      Else
        Print 'Discop wrongly called'   /* error */
        Stop
    Endif
End of Discop Subroutine
```

Create-segment does not allow us to create a segment if one is already open. It is necessary, therefore, to close an open segment after we have dealt with its data. (We do not have to say which segment to close because only one, Currentseg, can be open.) Close-segment (Table 11.10) does this.

Table 11.10 *Close-segment* subroutine

```
Subroutine Close-segment
/* Closes the currently open segment and all disc files */
    If Currentseg = 0 Then
      Print 'There is no open segment'
      Stop
    Endif
    Call Discop ('close', Currentseg)
    Currentseg = 0
End of Close-segment Subroutine
```

Table 11.11 *Putdata* subroutine

```
Subroutine Putdata (Num, Points)
Integer Num
Real Points
/* Writes data from array Points into an open file #1 */
Local Integer J
    Print#1, Num
    For J = 1 to Num
        Print#1, Points (J, 1), Points (J, 2)
    Next J
End of Putdata subroutine
```

We need a further routine to put information onto the disc files and another to retrieve it. Putdata (Table 11.11) and Getdata (Table 11.12) perform these tasks. They are device dependent and require tailoring to suit the disc operating commands of your system.

Table 11.12 *Getdata* subroutine

```
Subroutine Getdata (Num, Points)
Integer Num
Real Points
/* Reads Points data from an open file #1 */
Local Integer J
    While Not EOF(1)  /* Do not read beyond end of file */
        Input#1, Num
        For J = 1 to Num
            Input#1, Points (J, 1), Points (J, 2)
        Next J
    Endwhile
End of Getdata subroutine
```

Exercises

11.1 Using the drawing primitives of your system in place of MOVE and DRAW, code the Polyline subroutine and test it with different sets of Xarray and Yarray. Do this with a program based on Table 11.4 using the Set-window, Set-wsviewport and Makescales subroutines you prepared for Exercises 10.3 and 10.5.

11.2 Code the Hatch subroutine of Table 11.5 and use it to fill polygons with various patterns. Try to catch it out with shapes of some complexity. In particular, hatch the polygon described by the co-ordinate pairs (10,0), (40,60), (70,0), (0,40), (80,40) and (10,0). Hatch fills various parts of this self-intersecting polygon in what is considered to be the 'standard' way. Is it what you expected? If not, what other way would be logical?

11.3 By using closely-spaced horizontal lines (one pixel apart for screen display), show that Hatch can be used to provide solid area-fill. If your system has its own solid area-fill command, compare its performance with that of Hatch. If you have no solid area-fill, make another version of Hatch, say Fill, which omits the time-consuming rotation parts. Call this whenever area-fill is needed.

11.4 In the text we outline a method of area-fill which exploits the fact that some systems can tell if any of its pixels are illuminated. If yours is such a system, write a new subroutine to do area-fill which makes use of this facility.

11.5 If your system has built-in area-fill, find out whether it uses Polygon-fill or Seed-fill methods. List the advantages and disadvantages of each method. If Seed-fill is the technique, how do you ensure that the seed point you give the system by program is actually inside the polygon concerned? What happens if you ask the system to area-fill a polygon which is not quite complete? Does Hatch (or modified Hatch) give the same results in this case?

11.6 Some colour computer graphics systems have predefined sets of colours which you cannot alter. Others might have a default set on start-up but give you the opportunity to change if you want to. If your system is of the latter sort, check whether it expects you to use the RGB model or some other. It is not easy to work with RGB, so practice matching colours of all sorts of objects; in particular, try to get ranges of browns and greys. Bear in mind the hints on working with RGB given in the text.

11.7 Try and work out a subroutine to deal with anti-aliasing by the area method outlined in the text. Make the algorithm as efficient as you can. Is the method satisfactory? Have you any other ideas?

11.8 Good data handling facilities are important in computer graphics. Code and test the segment and storage routines given in the text remembering to use the disc-operating commands appropriate to your own system when you deal with Table 11.9. Putdata and Getdata are essential subroutines which you should code with the particular commands your system uses to allow the disc storage and retrieval of information.

11.9 Code and test subroutines Doros and Point. If your system has a simple command to plot a point, use this instead of Drawline. Can you think of ways to modify Doros in order to fill the circle or to draw ellipses?

12

Interaction

The subroutines we have given can be put into progams which simply take data and make drawings without further manual intervention. This is the non-interactive use of computer graphics. There are many occasions, though, when we wish to work interactively in order to perform the graphics tasks described in Chapter 2. To facilitate this interaction, we need to have subroutines which can take information from input devices and deal with it appropriately. There are two basic techniques of handling interaction and, to a certain extent, they depend on the characteristics of the input devices and the computer to be used.

The first technique is called **interrupt handling**. In this case, a signal is sent from an input device by the user to inform the processor that the device needs attention and that some input event is about to happen. The signal makes the program interrupt the task that it has currently in hand and sets the system in a state ready to receive data. In order to do this, the program must save the current state of the program before it deals with the input. When the event is over, the current state is restored and the interrupted task continues.

As we may have more than one input device connected to the system and it may be inconvenient to have interrupts occurring at certain times, we must be able to switch the devices on or off from within the program. This is a logical rather than a physical switching and is called *enabling* for on and *disenabling* for off. Event-driven interrupts are especially good for pick and button devices.

The second technique is known as **polling**. In this case, the program enters a loop and stays there waiting for the user to initiate some action on the input device, such as pressing a button or key. While in the loop, the system continually checks or 'polls' to see if the awaited event has happened. If it has, data are accepted and the program moves on. If it has not, polling continues. An example of polling occurs in BASIC when using the INPUT command. This causes a polling loop to be set up and the system to go on waiting until the RETURN key is pressed.

The effect of event-driven polling is that a program will only accept information when it is ready for it. Many small systems can only work in this mode and cannot do anything else while they are in a polling loop. We will assume that our graphics primitive, ACCEPT, is a polling command so we will only deal with polled events. We will also assume that, while in the polling mode, the system displays a tracking cross on the screen so that we can identify the notional position of the coordinates that ACCEPT will receive.

Locators

To give a location, we can point to a spot on a tablet or the screen (if we have a light pen) and ask the computer to accept the coordinates of this. To initiate the acceptance we must press a button and have to be in a subroutine which expects to receive locations. By entering new locations one after another, we can draw lines in a point-to-point fashion (Figure 12.1). To indicate that we have come to the end of the series of lines, we can either point to a specially designated part of the input surface or, if the locator device has

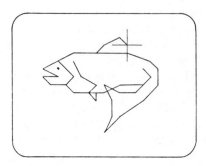

Figure 12.1 Tracking cross showing current pen position

Table 12.1 *Createlines* subroutine

```
Subroutine Createlines (N, Oarray)
Integer N
Real Oarray
/* Accepts the coordinates of up to Maxnum - 1 points from a locator and
displays lines connecting them. The resulting N pairs of coordinates are
stored in Oarray. When the locator flag, F, equals 2, or Y1 < YD (the lowest
part of the drawing area), the subroutine ends and this coordinate set is
ignored. YD should be globally defined outside the subroutine */
Global Integer YD
Local Integer Maxnum, J, F, X1, Y1
Local Real Temp, X,Y
   Maxnum = 100
   N = 0
   Dim Temp(Maxnum,2) /* temporary array storage */
   For J = 1 to Maxnum
     ACCEPT (F, X1, Y1)
     If F = 2 or Y1 < YD Then
       J = Maxnum + 1  /* ready to finish */
     Else
       N = N + 1  /* number of coordinate pairs */
       Call Convert (X1; X) /*to world coordinates */
       Call Convert (Y1; Y)
       Temp(J,1) = X
       Temp(J,2) = Y
       If J = 1 Then   /* do the drawing */
         MOVE (X1, Y1)
       Else
         DRAW (X1, Y1)
       Endif
     Endif
   Next J
/* Load Oarray with coordinates */
   Dim Oarray(N,2)
   For J = 1 to N
     Oarray(J,1) = Temp(J,1)
     Oarray(J,2) = Temp(J,2)
   Next J
End of Createlines Subroutine
```

more than one button, press the 'end this activity' button. The input coordinates we accept will be in device coordinates and we must convert these to world coordinates before using. A subroutine for accepting and drawing in this manner is shown in Table 12.1.

Picks and choices generally

In interactive mode, we frequently need to identify items on the screen by indicating them with the tracking cross and a pick device. These objects can be menu items or parts of a picture such as points, lines or whole segments.

Menu choice

To make a choice from a menu, which might consist of a matrix of rectangular cells such as Figure 12.2, we indicate a point (PX, PY) within the desired cell. Then, we check the coordinates of the chosen point against the boundaries of each rectangle. We can do this by looking at the coordinates (Xminr, Yminr, Xmaxr, Ymaxr) of each rectangle in turn and seeing if:

Xminr <PX and Xmaxr > PX and Yminr < PY and Ymaxr > PY

When this is true, we have found out which cell is being indicated. Searching in this way, however, is rather slow and does not exploit the fact that all the rectangles are of the same size and arranged in order. Given that the menu has the details shown in Figure 12.3, Menuchoice (Table 12.2) will find the cell in which (PX,PY) lies.

Having chosen an item from the menu, we could proceed to make

Figure 12.2   Typical screen menu

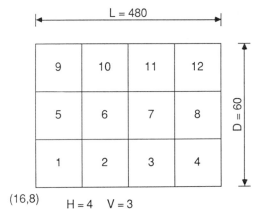

Figure 12.3 A menu layout

Table 12.2 *Menuchoice* subroutine

Subroutine Menuchoice (PX, PY; IDnum)
Integer PX, PY, IDnum
/* Returns a number, IDnum, indicating which menu rectangle has been
pointed at by coordinates (PX,PY). The menu has been globally defined by
its size L x D; the number of cells horizontally, H, and vertically, V; the
coordinates of its bottom left hand corner (X0,Y0). If IDnum = 0 then
(PX,PY) is not in the menu space. All dimensions are in device coordinates
*/
Local Integer NX, NY
Local Real SX, SY
  SX = L / H   /* width of menu cells */
  SY = D / V   /* height of menu cells */
  NX = **Int** ((PX − X0) / SX) + 1
  NY = **Int** ((PY − Y0) / SY) + 1
  IDnum = (NY −1) * H + NX
  If IDum > H * V **or** IDnum < 1 **Then**
    IDum = 0
  Endif
End of Menuchoice Subroutine

Table 12.3

```
/* Program fragment to draw lines with a locator */
   L = 480    /* menu details in device coordinates */
   D = 60
   X0 = 16
   Y0 = 8
   H = 4     /* menu has 12 cells */
   V = 3
   Flag = 0
   While Flag = 0 Do   /* until end flag set */
     ACCEPT (F, PX, PY)
     Call Menuchoice (PX, PY; IDN)
       Case of IDN:
       1: Call Createlines (Num, OA)  /* joined lines */
       2:                             /* next activity */
          .
          .
          .
      12: Flag = 1                    /* end */
       End of Case
   End while
/* End of program fragment */
```

a drawing with a combination of calls to Menuchoice and Createlines in the manner of Table 12.3.

Picking points

When we want to pick a point which is already displayed on the screen and included somewhere in an array, we have to ACCEPT the coordinates and check these against those in the array. It would be unreasonable to expect that we could indicate exactly the right coordinates when we point to the spot with a pick device. We will, however, be able to indicate roughly the position without any ambiguity and would expect the system to find the exact point for us from this indication. To do this we must define a region around the pick coordinates and search for a point which lies within it. This is the reverse of the menu picking problem when we have a point and wish to find the region in which it lies. Here we have a region and want to find the point (preferably only one) which lies in it.

The shape of the region around the pick point is of some importance. The best shape is a circle because its boundary is the same distance from the pick point throughout (Figure 12.4a). If we

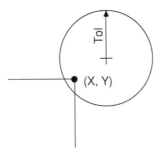

Figure 12.4a   Picking circle centred at (PX, PY) includes point (X, Y)

give the circle a radius of Tol, we can check if a point (X,Y) lies in it by seeing if

$$(PX - X)^2 + (PY - Y)^2 < Tol^2$$

for each point in the array.

A faster method is to define a square region whose sides are 2 * Tol long (Figure 12.4b). Then we need only check if:

$$Abs (PX - X) + Abs (PY - Y) < Tol.$$

Square regions, though, are not so intuitively easy to use (especially if we do not intend to display the region when we are picking – something we can only do conveniently if our system allows us to define our own tracking crosses).

Whichever shape of region we adopt, initially we would set Tol to some convenient amount by default. As more and more points appear in our drawing we would find it harder to pick individual

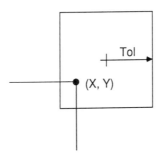

Figure 12.4b   Picking square centred at (PX, PY) includes point (X, Y)

points with this tolerance. When this happens, we must decrease the value of Tol to suit. Usually it would be sufficient to scale the decreases (or increases) in multiples of two. The routines to pick points and to change tolerances are left as exercises.

Picking lines

Picking lines requires rather more computation than picking points. If we have a set of lines whose endpoints are held in an array, we have to go through the array and check if the distance between a chosen point (PX,PY) and any line is less than some given distance, Tol, which defines a picking region (Figure 12.5). With a circular picking region and two endpoints defined by (XS,YS) and (XE,YE), the calculations we need are:

$$U = ((PX - XS) \cdot (YE - YS) - (PY - YS) \cdot (XE - XS))^2$$
$$L = (XE - XS)^2 + (YE - YS)^2$$

The line is chosen if $U / L < Tol^2$

In order not to have to perform this fairly complicated calculation for lines which could not possibly be candidates for the choice, we might first of all eliminate any where the picking region lies outside the endpoints of the line. We can therefore immediately reject a line if any of the following are true:

PX < Min (XS, XE) − Tol
PX > Max (XS, XE) + Tol
PY < Min (YS, YE) − Tol
PY > Max (YS, YE) + Tol

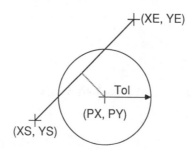

Figure 12.5   Using a picking circle to find a line by calculating its distance from (PX, PY)

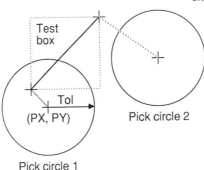

Figure 12.6 Picking lines with aid of test box (line is candidate for Pick circle 1 but not Pick circle 2)

What we have done here is to set up a test box around a line in the manner of Figure 12.6. If the pick point is not in this box, the line cannot be a candidate. However, if the point does lie within the box, we still have to check that the line is the likely choice as there may be others that share the space.

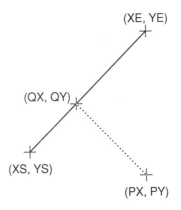

Figure 12.7 Point (QX, QY) is nearest point to (PX, PY) on line from (XS, YS) to (XE, YE)

Sometimes we need not only to identify the line itself but also the point on it which is nearest the pick point (Figure 12.7). A procedure for doing this is:

1 Identify the line.

2 Find the value of T for the point Q on the line by using the equation:

$$T = ((XE - PX) * (XE - XS) + (YE - PY) * (YE - YS))/L$$
where L is defined as above.

3 Use this value of T in the parametric form of the line to locate (QX,QY), the closest point.

The method is embodied in Table 12.4.

Table 12.4 *Picklinept* subroutine

```
Subroutine Picklinept (N, Larray, Dtol, PXD, PYD; Num, WX, WY)
Integer N, Num, Dtol,PXD, PYD
Real Larray WX, WY
/* Searches through Larray containing N coordinate sets of line endpoints
to find the first line which is within a distance, Dtol, from the pick point
(PXD,PYD). It returns Num, indicating the array position of the start point
of the line and (WX,WY), the world coordinates of the point on the line
closest to (PXD,PYD). If Num = 0, there are no lines meeting the condition
and WX, WY are undefined. PXD, PYD, and Dtol are all in device coordinates.
Larray is in world coordinates */
    Local Integer J
    Local Real PX, PY, Tol, XS, XE, XD, XL, YS, YE, YD, YL, U, UU, L, T
    Call Convert (PXD; PX)      /* to world coordinates */
    Call Convert (PYD; PY)
    Call Convert (Dtol; Tol)
    Num = 0
    For J = 1 to N -1
        XS = Larray(J,1)      /* start of line */
        YS = Larray(J,2)
        XE = Larray(J+1,1)   /* end of line */
        YE = Larray(J+1,2)
    /* Preliminary box check would go here */
        XD = XE - XS
        YD = YE - YS
        XL = PX - XS
        YL = PY - YS
        U = XL * YD - YL * YD
        UU = U * U
        L = XD * XD + YD * YD
    /* do tolerance check */
```

```
    If UU / L < = Tol * Tol Then
        T = (XL * XD + YL * YD) / L
    If T > - 0 and T < - 1 Then
        WX = XS + T * XD
        WY = YS + T * YD
        Num = J
        J = N   /* exit: line found */
    Endif
 Endif
Next J
End of Picklinept Subroutine
```

Picking segments

We can pick a segment by identifying one of its lines found by searching as we did in Picklinept. If there are many segments and many lines this might be a slow process. It can be speeded up if the segment table also stores the coordinates (Bxmin, Bxmax, Bymin, Bymax) of boxes which surround each segment as in Figure 12.8. Using these boxes we can make a preliminary check to see if a segment is a likely candidate before looking at its constituent parts. It may be that a segment has been transformed by rotation, translation or scaling when it was placed on the screen. If so, the surrounding box coordinates must be similarly treated before the search can begin.

To check whether a pick point (PX, PY) is in a transformed box, we use the transformed coordinates (TBXmin, TBXmax, TBYmin, TBYmax) as in Figure 12.9. The segment is a possible candidate if

PX > TBXmin and PK < TBXmax and PY > TBYmin and
PY < TBYmax

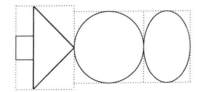

Figure 12.8   Segments surrounded by bounding boxes

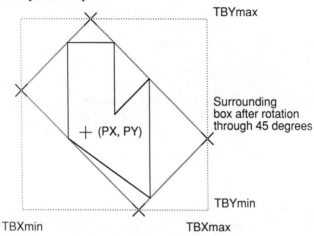

Figure 12.9   Coordinate values of the bounding box change after rotation

As only visible segments can be picked, we must first check the visibility attribute before making the box test; we then use Picklinept on the remaining segment arrays.

To find the minimum and maximum values of an array, we use the routine given in Table 12.5.

Table 12.5   *Extremes subroutine*

```
Subroutine Extremes (N, OA; X0, Y0, X9, Y9)
Integer N
Real OA, X0, X9, Y0, Y9
/* Finds the minimum values, X0, Y0, and the maximum values, X9, Y9, of
the array OA of N points */
Local Integer J
  X0 = OA(1,1)   /* assume that the first is min and max */
  Y0 = OA(1,2)
  X9 = OA(1,1)
  Y9 = OA(1,2)
  For J = 2 to N
    If OA(J,1) < X0 Then
      X0 = OA(J,1)   /* new min X */
    Else
      If OA(J,1) > X9 Then
        X9 = OA(J,1)   /* new max X */
```

```
        Endif
      Endif
      If OA(J,2) < Y0 Then
        Y0 = OA(J,2)   /* new min Y */
      Else
        If OA(J,2) > Y9 Then
          Y9 = OA(J,2)   /* new max Y */
        Endif
      Endif
    Next J
  End of Extremes subroutine
```

Exercises

12.1 If your system has a mouse, joystick, digitising tablet or other locator, use it in company with the subroutine Createlines to make drawings and store data points. You will need to substitute the particular commands your system uses in place of ACCEPT, MOVE and DRAW.

12.2 Use the subroutine Menuchoice and your input device as a Choice to let you choose items from a menu of ten or so on the screen or tablet. Test the efficiency of Menuchoice by pointing to areas outside the menu as well as inside.

12.3 Write, code and test subroutines for picking points and changing tolerances using the techniques outlined in the text. In particular test whether there is any worthwhile gain in speed of interaction by using a pick square (Figure 12.4b) rather than a pick circle (Figure 12.4a). Even if there is a speed gain, is the pick square as easy to use as the pick circle? If it is possible to define cursors with your system, pick points with the pick circle or square displayed. Does this result in better interaction than picking with the normal cursor? Think of other improvements.

12.4 Code the Picklinept subroutine and use it to detect lines and closest points. When you have fully tested the subroutine, use it and the point picking subroutine of Exercise 12.3 to pick segments. Try full-scale searching of the data for a complicated drawing first and then the surrounding box method given in the text to see whether any significant time savings can be achieved.

12.5 Identifying which segment is being picked after it has been through a number of transformations is not a trivial task. We have suggested a way of doing this in the text. Can you think of other ways that might be more effective?

12.6 Even with small pick circles, it may be that there is more than one point which could be a candidate for identification. Which point should be identified: the first in the list of points or the last one created? Should you print a message telling the user that the pick is ambiguous? Think about the possibilities and list the advantages and disadvantages of all of these. In particular, devise a method of indicating to the user that there are no points within the pick circle. Remember, with most computers it is possible to make sounds so these might be used in place of, or in addition to, visual warnings.

13

Modelling: 3-D Rectilinear Objects

Three-dimensional objects can be described in a variety of ways some of which are analogous to the two-dimensional cases. For example, we can use points and lines to indicate vertices and edges of polyhedra. Thus, as illustrated in Figure 13.1, a cube might have its eight corners located at the positions:

(0,0,0), (1,0,0), (1,0,1), (0,0,1)
(0,1,0), (1,1,0), (1,1,1), (0,1,1)

We can number these coordinate triples from 1 to 8 and make a list of the endpoints of the lines which comprise the twelve edges thus:

(1,2), (2,3), (3,4), (4,1), (1,5), (5,6)
(6,2), (6,7), (7,3), (7,8), (8,4), (8,5)

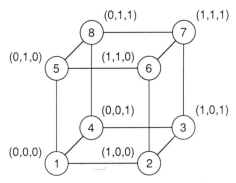

Figure 13.1   Cube showing coordinates of corners

176   *Computer Graphics*

If you have difficulty visualising these points and lines, it is worth getting a small box and marking the corners with their coordinates and numbers.

The description given is satisfactory for some cases but is not adequate for others. In particular, there is not enough information in it to tell us anything about the faces of the cube – something that we will need to know if, for example, we intend to colour them in. One way to deal with this requirement is to make an ordered list of the coordinates of the bounding corners of each face. We should do this in a consistent fashion; say, clockwise when each face is viewed from the outside. A systematic method is not just to ensure that all the points are properly included – although it certainly helps in this. The main reason is to allow us to determine in which direction a face is pointing after rotation.

```
4   /* south face */
0, 0, 0,  0, 1, 0,  1, 1, 0,  1, 0, 0
4   /* east face */
1, 0, 0,  1, 1, 0,  1, 1, 1,  1, 0, 1
4   /* north face */
1, 0, 1,  1, 1, 1,  0, 1, 1,  0, 0, 1
4   /* west face */
0, 0, 1,  0, 1, 1,  0, 1, 0,  0, 0, 0
4   /* top */
0, 1, 0,  0, 1, 1,  1, 1, 1,  1, 1, 0
4   /* bottom */
0, 0, 0,  1, 0, 0,  1, 0, 1,  0, 0, 1
0   /* end */
```

Because this description uses each coordinate set in triplicate, it is wasteful in storage particularly if many or more complicated objects are described. More importantly, each point has to pass through any transformation routines three times. It is, however, simple to understand and create but, as in the 2-D case, it is probably better to keep the points and lines in separate lists thus:

```
/* Vertex list of cube */

8    /* number of vertices */
0, 0, 0,  1, 0, 0,  1, 0, 1,  0, 0, 1
0, 1, 0,  1, 1, 0,  1, 1, 1,  0, 1, 1
```

```
/* Face list - clockwise ordering */
4   /* south face */
1, 5, 6, 2
4   /* east face */
2, 6, 7, 3           .
4   /* north face */
3, 7, 8, 4
4  /* west face */
4, 8, 5, 1
4   /* top */
5, 8, 7, 6
4   /* bottom */
1, 2, 3, 4
0   /* end */
```

By means of these two lists, we can pass the coordinates for each point through the transformation routines just once and still know which edges and faces are connected.

It helps in the description of convex polyhedra to remember that the numbers of vertices, edges and faces are interrelated by a simple formula known as Euler's Polyhedron Theorem. This says that the:

No. of vertices + No. of faces − No. of edges = 2

Thus, to check that we have given enough information to describe a cube, we can see that the number of vertices in our list is 8 and the number of faces is 6, therefore we need $8 + 6 - 2 = 12$ edges. We have, in fact, listed 24 edges in our faces list but each one is given twice – once in one direction and once in the opposite. The correct numbers elements have thus been listed.

Planes

When we considered 2-D objects in Chapter 3, we showed that any two different points uniquely defined a line and that the coordinates of points on this line were related by the formula:

$$AX + BY + C = 0$$

In the 3-D case, we can note that any two lines uniquely define a plane (Figure 13.2) and that all the points on this plane are related by the formula:

$$AX + BY + CZ + D = 0$$

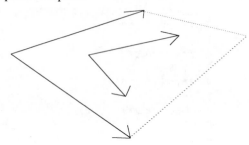

Figure 13.2   Any two lines define a plane

If we assume that these two lines run from a common starting point $(X2,Y2,Z2)$, and that their endpoints are $(X1,Y1,Z1)$ and $(X3,Y3,Z3)$ as in Figure 13.3, we can derive the coefficients A, B, C and D by the formulae:

$$XA = X1 + X2$$
$$XB = X2 + X3$$
$$XC = X3 + X1$$

$$YA = Y1 + Y2$$
$$YB = Y2 + Y3$$
$$YC = Y3 + Y1$$

$$ZA = Z1 + Z2$$
$$ZB = Z2 + Z3$$
$$ZC = Z3 + Z1$$

$$A = (Y1 - Y2) * ZA + (Y2 - Y3) * ZB + (Y3 - Y1) * ZC$$
$$B = (Z1 - Z2) * XA + (Z2 - Z3) * XB + (Z3 - Z1) * XC$$
$$C = (X1 - X2) * YA + (X2 - X3) * YB + (X3 - X1) * YC$$
$$D = -(A * X1 + B * Y1 + C * Z1)$$

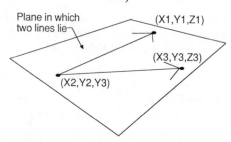

Figure 13.3   Two vectors in a plane

Note the symmetry in the relationships and that any three points will determine the plane providing they are not colinear (that is, they do not lie in one straight line).

Normals

In computer graphics it is often important to know the directions in which the sides of an object are facing. We can imagine a line sticking out of a particular face at right angles to the surface as in Figure 13.4. This line is known as the *surface normal* and the direction in which it is pointing determines the direction of the face.

A plane which has the coefficients A, B, C and D has a normal which runs from the point (XP,YP,ZP) to the point (A + XB, B + YP, C + ZP). Thus the plane described by the formula:

$$3 * X + 2 * Y + 6 * Z - 23 = 0$$

has a normal which runs from the surface point (3,4,1) to the point (9,6,7).

It frequently happens that we want the normal to be of length 1. We achieve this by dividing each coefficient, A, B and C, by the square root of the sum of the squares of A, B and C. Thus, if

$$L = \sqrt{(A^2 + B^2 + C^2)}$$

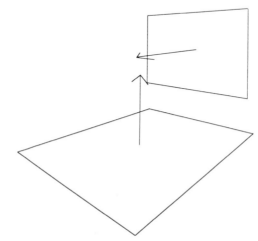

Figure 13.4 Normals to surfaces

then the unit normal at point (XP,YP,ZP) runs to the point

   (A/L + XP, B/L + YP, C/L + ZP).

For example, the unit normal at the point (3,4,1) to the plane whose coefficients are (3,2,6,−23) runs from (3,4,1) to (24/7,30/7,13/7).

For the normal to be pointing outwards from the front rather than inwards from the back depends on the way in which we have described the plane and this, in turn, depends on the order in which we have specified the three points which we used to determine the coefficients. If we put them in clockwise order, the normal points in one direction, if they are in anticlockwise order, the normal points in the opposite direction. We can see this if we use the points (3,1,4), (0,0,0) and (1,4,3) to define a plane. Putting them into the plane equation formulae in the order given, we obtain the coefficients (13,5,−11,0), which gives us a unit normal at (0,0,0) of (13,5,−11). Putting them in in the reverse order, we obtain the coefficients (−13,−5,11,0), which give us a normal at (0,0,0) of (−13,−5,11). These normals are in diametrically opposite directions.

Using our coordinate system and the plane equation formulae given above, an object whose faces are listed in clockwise order will have its normals pointing outwards. We will always describe our planes in clockwise order and exploit this ordering in a number of algorithms.

Normals and visibility

There is an alternative method of computing surface normals which does not require working out of the coefficients of the plane. This involves the vector cross product (Appendix 1). Given three points P1(X1,Y1,Z1), P2(X2,Y2,Z2) and P3(X3,Y3,Z3) all lying in a plane, we can draw vectors from P2 to P1 and from P2 to P3 as shown in Figure 13.5. The cross product of these two vectors, V1 and V3, gives us a new vector which is normal to the surface at P2. Once again, the order in which the points are given affects the direction of the normal. The cross product V1 × V3 gives a normal at P2 pointing in one direction and V3 × V1 gives a normal at P2 in the opposite direction. Thus (3,1,4) × (1,4,3) gives a normal at (0,0,0) of (−13,−5,11), and (1,4,3) × (3,1,4) gives a normal at

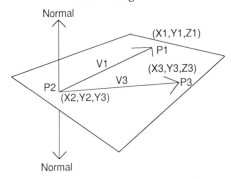

Figure 13.5   The vector cross-product

(0,0,0) of (13,5,−11). This means that, looking directly at a face, the points P1, P2 and P3 have to be given in a clockwise direction and the cross product must be V3 × V1 for the normal to point towards us.

We can exploit the directionality of the normal to determine whether we can see the faces of objects after they have been rotated. Obviously, in solid objects, only faces which have normals pointing roughly in our direction can be seen. A few moments experimentation with a pencil standing on a book will convince you that a surface points away from us if the angle between a line from our viewpoint and the normal is greater than 90 degrees or less than −90 degrees. This being so, we can check whether a particular plane can be seen by measuring the angle between our viewline and the surface normal where it touches the plane. Fortunately, vector algebra comes to our aid in doing this.

As is pointed out in Appendix 1, the dot product of two vectors can be used to find the angle between them. Specifically, the dot product produces the cosine of the angle between two vectors each of length 1. Cosines of angles lie in the range −1 and +1 and the cosines of angles between −90 degrees and +90 degrees lie in the range 0 to +1. To check the angle, then, we have to work out the unit normal to a surface and take its dot product with a vector of unit length pointing towards our viewpoint. If the value of this product is less than 0, we know that the plane is facing away from us. A subroutine to compute a vector of unit length given its start and endpoints is shown in Table 13.1.

Table 13.1   *Unitvec* subroutine

```
Subroutine Unitvec (XS, YS, ZS, XE, YE, ZE; XU, YU, ZU)
Real XS, XE, XU, YS, YE, YU, ZS, ZE, YU
/* Computes a vector of unit length running from (XS,YS,ZS) towards
(XE,YE,ZE) */
Local Real L1, L2, L3, UL
    L1 = XE - XS
    L2 = YE - YS
    L3 = ZE - ZS
    UL = Sqr (L1 * L1 + L2 * L2 + L3 * L3)
    XU = L1 / UL + XS
    YU = L2 / UL + YS
    ZU = L3 / UL + ZS
End of Unitvec Subroutine
```

A subroutine to compute the unit normal using the cross product method could be of the form shown in Table 13.2.

To compute the cosine of the angle between two vectors of unit length we can use the Dot subroutine – which should be coded as a function if your system permits (Table 13.3).

Armed with these routines, we can check whether any plane

Table 13.2   *Normal* subroutine

```
Subroutine Normal (X1, Y1, Z1, X2, Y2, Z2, X3, Y3, Z3; XN, YN, ZN)
Real X1, X2, X3, XN, Y1, Y2, Y3, YN, Z1, Z2, Z3, ZN
/* Computes the unit normal at (X2, Y2, Z2). Assumes that the points are
listed in a clockwise direction when looking at the face */
Local Real XA, XB, XX, YA, YB, YY, ZA,ZB, ZZ
    XA = X1 - X2
    YA = Y1 - Y2
    ZA = Z1 - Z2
    XB = X3 - X2
    YB = Y3 - Y2
    ZB = Z3 - Z2
/* Take the cross product */
    XX = YB * ZA - ZB * YA  + X2
    YY = XA * ZB - XB * ZA  + Y2
    ZZ = XB * YA - XA * YB  + Z2
/* Make unit length */
    Call Unitvec ( X2, Y2, Z2, XX, YY, ZZ; XN, YN, ZN)
End of Normal Subroutine
```

Table 13.3 *Dot* subroutine

```
Subroutine Dot (X1, Y1, Z1, X2, Y2, Z2, X3, Y3, Z3; Csn)
Real X1, X2, X3, Y1, Y2, Y3, Z1, Z2, Z3, Csn
/* Computes the cosine of the angle between two vectors of unit length
sharing the common point (X2, Y2, Z2) */
Local Real XA, XB, YA, YB, ZA, ZB
    XA = X1 - X2
    YA = Y1 - Y2
    ZA = Z1 - Z2
    XB = X3 - X2
    YB = Y3 - Y2
    ZB = Z3 - Z2
/* Take dot product */
    Csn = XA * XB + YA * YB + ZA * ZB
End of Subroutine Dot
```

described by vertices listed in the clockwise direction can be seen from a viewpoint, as Table 13.4 shows.

The results of this are $XN = 0.732467$, $YN = 0.281718$, $ZN = -0.61978$, $XU = 0.19518$, $YU = 0.09759$, $ZU = -0.9759$, $Csn = 0.775299$, Visible. Using the same plane but a viewpoint of $(-3,0,-3)$, gives the results $XU = -0.7071$, $YU = 0$, $ZU = -0.7071$, $Csn = -0.079681$, Invisible.

Table 13.4

```
/* Program segment to check visibility of a plane described by vertices
listed clockwise. The program uses three points P1(X1,Y1,Z1),
P2(X2,Y2,Z2), P3(X3,Y3,Z3) which must not lie in a straight line. The
coordinates of the particular plane being tested are P1(3,1,4), P2(0,0,0),
P3(1,4,3). The viewpoint is situated at (2,1,-10) */
/* Calculate normal */
    Call Normal (3, 1, 4, 0, 0, 0, 1, 4, 3; XN, YN, ZN)
/* Calculate unit vector from P2 to viewpoint */
    Call Unitvec (0, 0, 0, 2, 1, -10; XU, YU, ZU)
/* Calculate the dot product of the unit normal and unit vector */
    Call Dot (XU, YU, ZU, 0, 0, 0, XN, YN, ZN; Csn)
/* Check visibility */
    If Csn > 0 Then
        Visible
    Else
        Invisible
    Endif /* End of program segment */
```

There are good reasons why we will normally place our viewpoint on the negative Z-axis. This means that the coordinates of the viewpoint are (0,0,−D), where D is the distance of the viewpoint from the origin.

Boundary representations of objects

In choosing to describe our objects in terms of the points, lines and properly orientated faces that make them up, we are using what can be called a *boundary representation* (Figure 13.6). This is a simple representation – perhaps the simplest unambiguous one – and can deal with many of the objects we want to draw. It is, however, a tedious and error-prone business to set up such a description. With some shapes, we have no alternative but to work out the coordinates, edges and planes laboriously by hand: others, fortunately, lend themselves to more automatic descriptions.

Two forms, in particular, fall into this category:

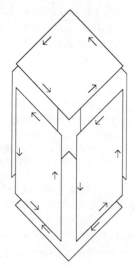

Figure 13.6 Boundary representation of a rectangular prism made up of faces

1 Those that have the same cross-sections throughout their lengths (Figure 13.7). Shapes like these can be thought of as

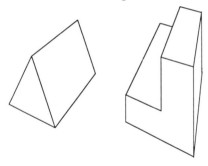

Figure 13.7   Extruded sections

being 'extruded' through a die of the given cross-section and
then cut to the appropriate lengths.

2   Those that are solids of revolution (Figure 13.8). These have a
cross-section that can be 'swept' around an axis through 360
degrees to complete the form.

Figure 13.8   Rotated form (smooth shaded)

Extruded forms

Solids of the first type can be generated by a subroutine such as
Extrude (Table 13.5). This creates the arrays we need from details
of the cross-section given in the X–Y plane together with the depth
in the Z-direction (with the front face at Z = 0). We make our
original description with the object in this 'canonical' position and
then transform its coordinates to the actual position, size and
orientation we require by means of translations, scalings and rotations in the usual way.

Table 13.5   *Extrude* subroutine

```
Subroutine Extrude(Num, Arry, Depth; N, Points, Slabs, Faces)
Integer Num, N
Real Arry, Depth, Points, Slabs, Faces
/* Creates the data for an extruded shape described by Arry (Num,2).
   The resulting endpoints are put in array Points (N,3) and the point
   indexes in arrays Slabs (2,Num+1) and Faces (Num,5) */
Local Integer J
Dim Points (2*Num,3), Slabs (2,Num+1), Faces (Num,5)
For J = 1 to Num           /* assign the points array */
   Points (J ,1) = Arry (J,1)
   Points (J+Num,1) = Arry (J,1)
   Points (J,2) = Arry (J,2)
   Points (J+Num,2) = Arry (J,2)
   Points (J,3) = 0
   Points (J+Num,3) = Depth
Next J
/* first deal with end faces and put point indexes into slabs arrays */
For J = 1 to Num
   Slabs (1,J ) = J
   Slabs (2,J ) = 2 * Num-(i-1)
Next J
   Slabs (1,Num+1) = 1
   Slabs (2,Num+1) = 2 * Num
/* now deal with Num-1 other faces */
For J = 1 to Num-1
   Faces(J,1) = Num + J
   Faces(J,2) = Num + J + 1
   Faces(J,3) = 1 + J
   Faces(J,4) = J
   Faces(J,5) = Num + J
Next J
/* finally deal with last face */
   Faces(Num,1) = 2 * Num
   Faces(Num,2) = Num + 1
   Faces(Num,3) = 1
   Faces(Num,4) = Num
   Faces(Num,5) = 2 * Num
End of Extrude subroutine
```

You should note that objects with complicated cross-sections make quite large arrays. A body with a 20-sided cross-section will need a 40 × 4 coordinate array and a line list of 164 entries in addition to the original description array of 20 × 2. A cylinder of 72 sides will need a 144 × 4 coordinate array and a line list of 580 entries as well as the original array of 72 × 2. If arrays of these sizes present problems, we can assume that the object occupies a whole segment on its own and, using the methods of Chapter 11, write the information to disc as soon as it is created. The line information can then be read off disc into a temporary small array for each plane as it is needed. If no disc is available, we cannot conveniently store the coordinates and we must draw each face as it is created.

Rotated forms

We can also easily describe quite complicated symmetrical forms by sweeping a profile through 360 degrees in steps of 360/n degrees (where n is the number of facets on the form as in Figure 13.9). After systematically defining all the points of the vertices of the shape, we then list the edges of one facet and replicate this for all the others. Once again it is important to ensure that the edges of the faces of each polygon are listed in a clockwise order to enable other subroutines to calculate the outward normals. It is then possible to draw in perspective only those faces which can actually be seen. Appendix 2 gives an Apple Macintosh program to do rotational sweeping.

Although the Extrude subroutine will cope with the description of simple shapes like rectangular boxes as well as more complicated

Figure 13.9   Rotated form (faceted)

forms, the rectangular box is such a frequent requirement that it is worth having a special fast routine just to set up the coordinates and faces for this. Once again, we would define the box in a canonical position and then transform its coordinates to the correct position, orientation and size when we need to. Thus it is sufficient to describe a unit cube centred about the origin in order to deal with any box.

Exercises

13.1 In this chapter we have suggested ways to represent the coordinates and faces of 3-D shapes. List the advantages and disadvantages of each method and try to think of some different ones. Remember that any representation must balance user effort, computation and storage requirements with adequacy of description. In particular, the representation must be *unambiguous*, that is to say, any given instance of a representation must describe only one shape.

13.2 Test Euler's Polyhedron theorem on shapes you see around you. Are there shapes on which the formula breaks down? In the form given it will not work with shapes with holes. Try to think of a way to modify the formula so that it can take care of such shapes (this is quite difficult, but it can be done). What about spheres and cylinders?

13.3 Write a subroutine incorporating the method we have given to determine the coefficients of the plane equation containing the three points P1 = (X1,Y1,Z1), P2 = (X2,Y2,Z2) and P3 = (X3,Y3,Z3). Remember to incorporate a check to deal with points which all lie in a straight line. Use the subroutine to check the following results:

P1 = (2,4,6), P2 = (0,0,0), P3 = (5,2,7)
  A = −16, B = −16, C = 16, D = 0
P1 = (5,5,5), P2 = (−2,7,0), P3 = (0,0,1)
  A = −33, B = −3, C = 45, D = −45
P1 = (0,0,0), P2 = (10,4,7), P3 = (1,2,3)
  A = −2, B = −23, C = 16, D = 0
P1 = (1,1,1), P2 = (4,1,0), P3 = (5,1,2)
  A = 0, B = −7, C = 0, D = 7
P1 = (1,1,1), P2 = (2,1,3), P3 = (3,1,5)
  Colinear points: no single plane

13.4 Note that the values of A,B,C and D are not unique. Any values having the same proportions will do. Thus the plane equation coefficients of the first question can be expressed as (−1,−1,1,0) after dividing through by 16 or even (1,1,−1,0) after dividing through by −16. Thus the plane equation is of the form: X + Y − Z = 0. What do these results tell you about a plane which passes through the origin? (Hint: the value of D is significant.) Does what you've learned explain why the coefficient, D, is not used to calculate the normal?

13.5 Use the results of Exercise 13.3 to check that the normals at the points P2 for each of the planes are as follows:

P2 = (0,0,0)   PN = (−16,−16,16)
P2 = (−2,7,0)   PN = (−35,4,45)
P2 = (10,4,7)   PN = (8,−19,23)
P2 = (4,1,0)   PN = (4,−6,0)

13.6 Show that the unit normals for the given planes at these points are:
from (0,0,0) to (−1,−1,1), UN = (−0.57735, −0.57735, 0.57735)
from (−2,7,0) to (−34,4,45), UN = (−2.59051, 6.94632, 0.805242)
from (10,4,7) to (8,−19,23), UN = (9.9288, 3.18118, 7.56962)
from (4,1,0) to (4,−6,0), UN = (4,0,0)

Because of the way the unit normal is calculated, it should come as no surprise to you that, in most cases, its components will be decimal numbers rather than integers. What can you tell about the plane whose unit normal is (4,0,0)?

13.7 Use your subroutines to convince you that the order in which you give the three points matters and that, if this is reversed, the normal will point in the opposite direction. Before making the last calculation – the one with unit normal (4,0,0) – guess what the result should be. (Hint: a sketch will help.)

13.8 Appendix 1 gives an alternative way of working out the surface normal via the vector cross product and this is incorporated in Table 13.2. Code the subroutine Normal and use it to check the results of Exercise 13.5. Remember here too, the points have to be given to the subroutine in a consistent order and that the vector running from (X0,Y0,Z0) to (X9,Y9,Z9) is (X9−X0,Y9−Y0,Z9−Z0). Confirm that, to obtain the same results as Exercise 13.5, the points have to be given in the opposite order.

13.9 Using your coded version of Dot, confirm that the cosine of the angle between the unit vectors (−0.57735, −0.57735, 0.57735) and (0,0,−1) is −0.57735. As the first unit vector is one normal to the plane X + Y − Z = 0, is this plane visible or invisible from point (0,0,−1)?

13.10 Code the subroutine Extrude and use it to describe the points and planes of various shapes. Modify the Macintosh program given in Appendix 2 to suit your own computer and use this to make forms which are rotationally symmetrical.

13.11 Write, code and test a box subroutine. Check it against the results obtained by extruding a rectangular cross-section.

14

3-D Transformations

In 3-D, the transformations we can apply are translation, rotation, scaling and shearing as in the 2-D case. In addition, there is another: the perspective transformation, taking us from 3-D to 2-D in a way which allows us to picture the appearance of 3-D objects from a viewpoint.

Translation

To translate the point (Xold,Yold,Zold,1) by amounts, Xmv, Ymv and Zmv, we use the matrix, T:

$$T = \begin{pmatrix} 1 & 0 & 0 & 0 \\ 0 & 1 & 0 & 0 \\ 0 & 0 & 1 & 0 \\ Xmv & Ymv & Zmv & 1 \end{pmatrix}$$

so that

$$(Xnew,Ynew,Znew,1) = (Xold,Yold,Zold,1) * T$$
$$= (Xold + Xmv, \quad Yold + Ymv, \quad Zold + Zmv, 1)$$

Rotation

In the 2-D case, only one rotation transformation was necessary – the one in the X–Y plane about an imaginary Z-axis. In 3-D, on the other hand, we have three axes about which rotation can take place. (Rotation about any arbitrary line can be achieved by compounding shifts and rotations about these axes.)

Rotation by an angle A about the negative Z-axis – equivalent to the 2-D rotation we have already dealt with – is given by the application of Rz.

$$Rz = \begin{pmatrix} C & S & 0 & 0 \\ -S & C & 0 & 0 \\ 0 & 0 & 1 & 0 \\ 0 & 0 & 0 & 1 \end{pmatrix}$$

where C = Cos (A) and S = Sin (A) as before.

Thus,

$$(Xnew, Ynew, Znew, 1) = (Xold, Yold, Zold, 1) * Rz$$
$$= (Xold * C - Yold * S, Xold * S + Yold * C, Zold, 1)$$

Rotation about the positive X-axis is given by applying Rx.

$$Rx = \begin{pmatrix} 1 & 0 & 0 & 0 \\ 0 & C & -S & 0 \\ 0 & S & C & 0 \\ 0 & 0 & 0 & 1 \end{pmatrix}$$

Thus,

$$(Xnew, Ynew, Znew, 1) = (Xold, Yold, Zold, 1) * Rx$$
$$= (Xold, \quad Yold * C + Zold * S, \quad Zold * C - Yold * S, 1)$$

Rotation about the positive Y-axis is given by applying Ry.

$$Ry = \begin{pmatrix} C & 0 & S & 0 \\ 0 & 1 & 0 & 0 \\ -S & 0 & C & 0 \\ 0 & 0 & 0 & 1 \end{pmatrix}$$

Thus,

$$(Xnew, Ynew, Znew, 1) = (Xold, Yold, Zold, 1) * Ry$$
$$= (Xold * C - Zold * S, \quad Yold, \quad Xold * S + Zold * C, 1)$$

When we use these rotations with a positive angle, the following effects occur if we are standing on the negative Z-axis:

Rx: the object tilts towards us
Ry: the right hand side of the object swings away
Rz: the object tilts over in an anticlockwise direction.

To set up the appropriate matrix, we use the single subroutine Rotmat given in Table 14.1.

Table 14.1   *Rotmat* subroutine

```
Subroutine Rotmat (Axstr, A; Mtrx)
String Axstr
Real A, Mtrx
/* Creates a rotation matrix, Mtrx, for angle A in degrees. The axis about
which rotation is to take place is determined by setting Axstr to 'x','y' or
'z' */
Local Integer H, J
Local Real C, S
Dim Mtrx(4,4)
    A = A * PI / 180
    C = Cos(A)
    S = Sin(A)
    For H = 1 to 4   /* initialise matrix */
        For J = 1 to 4
            If H = J Then
                Mtrx(H,J) = 1
            Else
                Mtrx(HJ) = 0
            Endif
        Next J
    Next H
    Case of Axstr:
        'x': Mtrx(2,2) = C
            Mtrx(2,3) = -S
            Mtrx(3,2) = S
            Mtrx(3,3) = C
```

```
'y': Mtrx(1,1) = C
      Mtrx(1,3) = S
      Mtrx(3,1) = -S
      Mtrx(3,3) = C
'z': Mtrx(1,1) = C
      Mtrx(1,2) = S
      Mtrx(2,1) = -S
      Mtrx(2,2) = C
End of Rotmat subroutine
```

Scaling

To scale the position of a point by the amounts Xsc, Ysc, Zsc, we use:

$$S = \begin{pmatrix} Xsc & 0 & 0 & 0 \\ 0 & Ysc & 0 & 0 \\ 0 & 0 & Zsc & 0 \\ 0 & 0 & 0 & 1 \end{pmatrix}$$

This gives:

$$(Xnew, Ynew, Znew, 1) = (Xold, Yold, Zold, 1) * S$$
$$= (Xold * Xsc, Yold * Ysc, Zold * Zsc, 1)$$

Concatenation

As in the 2-D case, we can apply the matrices for translation, rotation and scaling consecutively to the coordinates or concatenate them into one and apply this. (Alternatively, we can use the explicit transformation formulae if we do not wish to bother with matrices at all.) If we choose concatenation, we will need a subroutine to multiply together two matrices in order to produce a third. Matmult will serve for this. Note that the order in which we apply the matrices is very important: Mtrx1 × Mtrx2 is rarely the same as Mtrx2 × Mtrx1. For example, if we first rotate the point (3,3,3,1) through 30 degrees about the X-axis and then 30 degrees about the Y-axis, we arrive at the point (2.049,4.098,2.4509,1). This is equivalent to applying M3 to the point (3,3,3,1) after calling Matmult (Rx, Ry; M3). If the rotation is first 30 degrees about the Y-axis and

Table 14.2 *Matmult* subroutine

```
Subroutine Matmult (M1, M2; M3)
Real M1, M2, M3
/* Multiplies two 4 x 4 matrices to give a third */
Local Integer H, J, K
Local Real Temp
Dim M3(4,4)
   For H= 1 to 4
      For J = 1 to 4
         Temp = 0
         For K = 1 to 4
            Temp = Temp + M1(H,K) * M2(K,J)
         Next K
         M3(H,J) = Temp
      Next J
   Next H
End of Matmult subroutine
```

then 30 degrees about the X-axis, we get $(1.098, 4.647, 2.0489, 1)$. This is equivalent to applying M3 after calling Matmult (Ry, Rx; M3). Thus the first parameter of Matmult indicates the first transformation to be performed and the second parameter, the second transformation (Table 14.2).

To apply a 4×4 transformation matrix to a set of coordinate vertices, we use Applymat (Table 14.3).

Table 14.3 *Applymat* subroutine

```
Subroutine Applymat (N, CA, Mat; N, OA)
Integer N
Real CA, Mat, OA
/* Multiplies each of the N homogeneous vectors in CA by the 4 x 4
transformation matrix, Mat. Puts new values in array, OA */
Local Integer H, J, K
Local Real Temp
Dim OA(N,4)
   For H = 1 to N
      For J = 1 to 4
         Temp = 0
         For K = 1 to 4
            Temp = Temp + CA(H,K) * Mat(K,J)
```

Next K
　　OA(H,J) = Temp
Next J
Next H
End of Applymat subroutine

Perspective

When we want to display objects with some degree of realism we must employ the techniques of perspective drawing. In conventional manual drawings, perspective relies on the correct positioning of vanishing points – the points from which we must draw all lines that are parallel to given planes (Figure 14.1). In computer graphics, as might be expected, we use a mathematical transformation rather than vanishing points to give us perspective. Like the other transformations we have encountered, we apply the perspective transformation to each vertex of the objects we wish to display but, unlike the others, this transformation converts every point in 3-D space to an appropriate position in 2-D space.

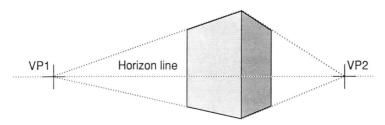

Figure 14.1 Conventional perspective showing vanishing points

To see how to derive the perspective transformation, we imagine looking at an object through a sheet of glass. We can mark a point on the sheet corresponding to each vertex in the scene (Figure 14.2). If we assume that our viewpoint is on the negative Z-axis at a distance of D world coordinate units from the origin and that the sheet of glass (technically called the *picture plane*) is in the X–Y plane at the origin as in Figure 14.3, we note that any point with coordinate, X, in the scene has the coordinate, XP, on the picture plane and that, by similar triangles,

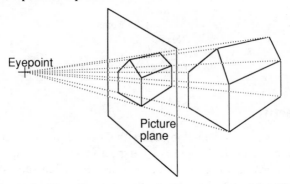

Figure 14.2 Lines drawn from scene to eye intersect picture plane

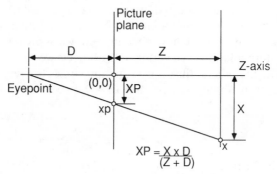

Figure 14.3 Position of point xp calculated by means of similar triangles

$$XP = X * D / (Z + D)$$
$$= X * 1 / ((Z / D) + 1)$$

The corresponding result for YP is,

$$YP = Y * D / (Z + D)$$
$$= Y * 1 / ((Z / D) + 1)$$

Because the picture plane is situated at $Z = 0$, all the Z-coordinates in the scene become zero in the picture. Thus, the X- and Y-positions on the picture plane depend on their X- and Y-positions in space together with a factor composed of the eye distance and the Z-positions in space. So that,

$$(Xnew, Ynew, Znew, 1) = (Xold * F, Yold * F, 0, 1)$$

where $F = 1 / ((Zold / D) + 1)$.

The matrix formulation of this is:

$$(Xnew, Ynew, Znew, 1) = (Xold, Yold, Zold, 1) * P$$

where $P =$
$$\begin{pmatrix} 1 & 0 & 0 & 0 \\ 0 & 1 & 0 & 0 \\ 0 & 0 & 0 & 1/D \\ 0 & 0 & 0 & 1 \end{pmatrix}$$

Applying P to (Xold, Yold, Zold, 1), we see that we get (Xold, Yold, 0, Zold/D + 1) but, from what we have learned about homogeneous coordinates, we know that this is equivalent to

$$(Xold * F, Yold * F, 0, 1)$$

where F is as previously defined.

To create a perspective view of an object, we perform the following:

1 Translate the object to the position we want relative to the viewpoint.
2 Rotate the object to present the desired faces.
3 Apply the perspective transformation to the coordinates of the vertices in order to map them onto the picture plane.
4 If needed, scale the result to make the drawing fit the drawing surface.
5 Display the result by connecting the transformed points with the correct lines (clipping as necessary).

Here again, we can perform the transformations separately or compounded into a single one. However, the translation, rotation and scaling matrices are the same for each object coordinate but the perspective matrix depends on the Z-coordinate value at each point. Thus it is probably more convenient to concatenate the translation and rotation matrices but to apply the scaling and perspective matrices separately – indeed, as the perspective transformation works only on the X- and Y-coordinates, you might find it better just to use the explicit formulae to convert to perspective rather than the matrix itself.

Changing the view

There are a number of different parameters we can alter to give us the best view of a scene:

1 With a window of fixed width, the viewpoint can be moved closer to or further from the picture plane. In other words, the value of D can be changed. A viewpoint relatively near the picture plane gives the effect of a photograph taken with a wide-angle lens: distant objects appear small; near ones appear large; angles of corners close to the viewpoint are very sharp (Figure 14.4). This is the technique for obtaining 'dramatic' views. Conversely, when the viewpoint is relatively far from the picture plane, the effect is that of a telephoto lens (Figure 14.5). For a more or less 'normal' appearance, the angle of view should be about 60 degrees. This means that the viewpoint should be roughly as far from the picture plane as the window is wide or high (whichever is the larger).

Similar effects are obtained if we keep the viewport distance fixed but vary the dimensions of the window. A relatively narrow window

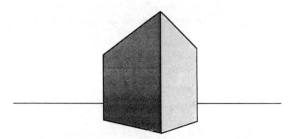

Figure 14.4 Perspective with wide-angle viewpoint

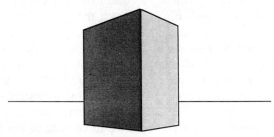

Figure 14.5 Perspective with 'telephoto' viewpoint

gives a narrow angle of view which produces a telephoto effect. A relatively wide window gives a wide-angle effect.

2 We can rotate objects about any of the axes. Normally, we will only want to turn the object about the Y-axis in order to favour particular faces (Figure 14.6). If, in addition, we want to favour the top or bottom of an object, we can rotate it through a positive angle in order to see the top, or a negative one in order to see the bottom. When we do this, as in Figure 14.7, we note that vertical lines no longer appear vertical. They, too, converge to a vanishing point and this adds to the dramatic effect if this is being sought. Rotation about the Z-axis tilts the object onto its side: except for special views, this will rarely be necessary.

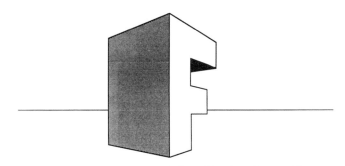

Figure 14.6   Letter rotated about Y-axis to favour side

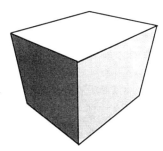

Figure 14.7   Tilting about the X-axis introduces a third vanishing point

3 We can move the objects relative to the picture plane. This means increasing or decreasing their coordinates by translation.

Increasing the X-coordinates shifts the objects to the right and decreasing shifts them to the left. Increasing the Y-coordinates moves the objects upwards – which favours bottom surfaces. Decreasing them moves the objects downwards and favours their tops. This is an alternative to rotating about the X-axis but without introducing convergence to vertical lines. Increasing the Z-coordinates moves the objects into the distance; decreasing them brings the objects nearer.

In decreasing the Z-coordinates, we must be careful not to put any part of the scene behind the viewpoint or unpredictable results will occur. If we are simulating the effect of travelling through a scene, it is inevitable that some parts of it will go behind the eye. In order to prevent undesirable consequences arising from this, we have to introduce another form of clipping: Z-clipping, which trims off any lines or parts of lines which pass behind the viewpoint. We must do this after rotations and translations but before perspective transformation.

Z-clipping

If, as before, the eye is at $-D$ on the Z-axis then we can clip to the plane $Z = -D$. To do this we need to check the Z-coordinates of each line to be drawn. Three possibilities arise as Figure 14.8 shows:

1   If the Z-coordinates of both endpoints are less than or equal to $-D$, then the whole of the line is behind the eyepoint and can be ignored.
2   If the Z-coordinates of both endpoints are greater than $-D$, then the whole of the line is in front of the eyepoint and need not be clipped at all.
3   Only if the Z-coordinate of one endpoint is greater than $-D$ and the other is less than or equal to it, need we perform clipping. In this case, it is sufficient to substitute the value $Z = -D$ into the equation of the line.

Thus, given the line going from P1: $(8,3,-10)$ to P2: $(0,4,10)$ with the eye at five units along the $-Z$ axis as in Figure 14.9, we see that the point P1 is behind the eye and the point P2 is in front. The parametric equations of this line are:

$X = 8 + t * (0 - 8) = 8 - 8 * t$
$Y = 3 + t * (4 - 3) = 3 + t$
$Z = -10 + t * (10 - -10) = -10 + 20 * t$

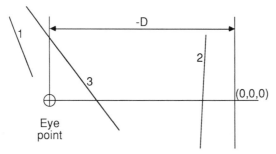

Figure 14.8 Z-Clipping of lines

Line 1 can be ignored as it is completely behind the eyepoint. Line 2 is visible and does not have to be z-clipped. Part of line 3 lies behind the eyepoint and must be clipped.

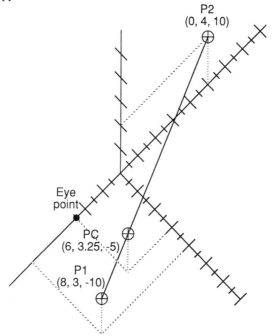

Figure 14.9 Clipping against the plane containing the eyepoint

Then, when $Z = -5$, $5 = 0.25$, so that, at $Z = -5$, $X = 6$ and $Y = 3.25$. This shows that the clipped line runs from PC: $(6, 3.25, -5)$ to P2: $(0, 4, 10)$ and that these are the points we should pass to the perspective subroutine.

Hidden lines and surfaces

If we describe our objects just in terms of points and lines, we can only draw them in wire-frame form (Figure 14.10). Such drawings are not very realistic and can be confusing for complex scenes although they are often quite acceptable for animation. (This is because even slight movement introduces parallax to give us clues about depth.) In order to establish a more convincing picture of solidity, we must use at least a minimum form of boundary representation describing points, lines and planes. By use of the technique outlined in Table 13.4, we can check each plane making up an object to ascertain if it faces the viewer and draw it if it can be seen.

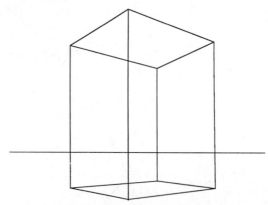

Figure 14.10   A wire-frame drawing

With single, convex objects (those having no depressions or protrusions – for example, such things as cubes or icosohedra), faces can be seen in their entirety or not at all. Thus, in these cases, it is sufficient first to do the visibility check and then to draw the visible faces to ensure an appearance of solidity (Figure 14.11). If, on the other hand, there is more than one object in the scene or if a single

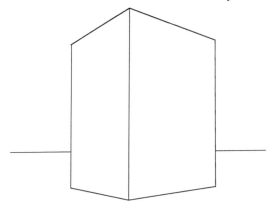

Figure 14.11   Solid faces hiding other parts

object is not convex – like the one in Figure 14.12 – surfaces which face the viewer might be wholly or partially obscured by other bodies or by parts of an object itself. We must make use of more elaborate techniques to cope with these cases.

The techniques we use will differ depending on whether we are drawing in line, depicting only the edges of planes, or with filled-in areas depicting the surfaces. In the former case, we have to tackle the hidden line problem; in the latter, the hidden surface problem. Surprisingly, it is easier to deal with hidden surfaces than with hidden lines.

One particularly simple approach to hidden surface removal is known as the painters' algorithm. It takes its name because of its resemblance to a possible way of painting pictures (although no

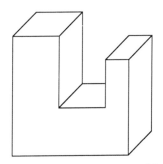

Figure 14.12   A non-convex object

artist actually uses such a quaint method). If we were painting a scene with oil colours, one way would be first to paint the background as if there were no objects in the scene at all. Then we could go on to paint the objects furthest away from us, and then the objects a little nearer, and so on until we finally delineate the objects nearest the eye. During this process we would be progressively adding complete objects to the scene according to their distance from us and, each time, we assume that there are no nearer objects to be shown. As we proceed, the closer objects would automatically obscure parts of the objects further away and, when we had finished, things would look in their proper order.

To translate this idea into computer terms, we must:

1   Remove from consideration all planes which face away from the viewpoint because these cannot possibly be seen. The technique given in Table 13.4 will deal with this.
2   Sort the remaining faces in order of distance from the viewpoint with the furthest at the head of the list.
3   Draw these faces with solid colour in list order.

Shading

We can add further to the realism of our solid-coloured drawings if we shade the faces of the objects we are drawing according to the amount of light that falls on them. Obviously, the sides of an object directly facing a light source appear brighter than those which have the light falling obliquely on them but, unfortunately, the degree of lightness is not directly related to the angle of the light. A law of physics known as Lambert's Law, however, tells us that the amount of light reflected from a point on a matt surface is proportional to the cosine of the angle between the light source and the normal to the surface at that point (Figure 14.13).

We have already learned in Chapter 13 that the cosine of the angle between two normal vectors is given by their dot product so, given that we know the position of a light source and the normal to a surface, we can readily calculate the lightness of the colour that we should render the surface. We can summarise this by the formula:

Illumination $= K * (N \cdot L)$

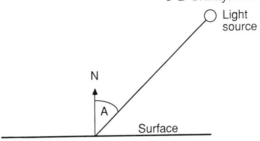

Figure 14.13 Illumination depends on the cosine of the angle between surface normal and light source

where K is a constant which we can change to control the exact values of the brightness we use and $(N \cdot L)$ is the dot product of the unit normal to a surface (N) and a unit vector pointing towards a light source (L). If the light source is fairly close to the surface, we can see from Figure 14.14 that L will be different at different points (this is one of the reasons why a table lamp does not illuminate the whole of your work surface evenly). If, however, the light source we are using is a long way from the surface – like the sun – we can assume that L is fixed for the whole scene. The advantage of this assumption is that, for any particular plane, we only need to

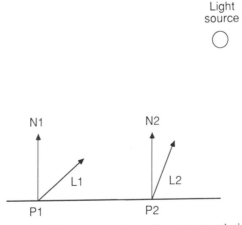

Figure 14.14 When light source is close, the vectors pointing towards it are different at different positions on the surface

calculate its unit normal and take the dot product with the fixed unit vector L to know what lightness to render the surface.

Lambert's Law deals with diffuse lighting (of the sort you get on an overcast day) and with matt surfaces. It also does not take into account the light that we get from the whole scene around us: the ambient light. It models the lighting conditions in outer space where there is no illumination from the sky but only from distant sources. The effect of rendering the surfaces of a computer graphics object with Lambert's Law lighting is to exaggerate the differences between surfaces pointing directly towards the light and those which are oblique to it. We can get over this defect by adding a fixed amount of illumination to deal with the ambient component. This leads to the formula:

Illumination = Ambient + K $*$ (N $\cdot$ L)

If we want also to vary the amount of illumination from the source (Isource), we can make the formula:

Illumination = Isource $*$ ambient factor + Isource $*$ K $*$ (N$\cdot$L)

Then if, say, we want our object to be illuminated by light in the proportions 20 per cent ambient and 80 per cent direct, we can use an ambient factor of 0.2 and K of 0.8.

In order to render scenes with highlights and reflective objects, we need to take into account other factors which are beyond the scope of this book (see Further Reading).

Exercises

14.1 Code and test the routines Rotmat, Matmult and Applymat. Use these to check the rotations of the point (3,3,3,1) given in the text. Try these with a number of different points to convince yourself that the order in which rotations are performed is vital.

14.2 Check whether or not it is quicker and easier to use explicit multiplications rather than matrix multiplications. Try this with and without translations. If you program in APL or in a version of BASIC which has matrix manipulation built in (as the original Dartmouth BASIC did), use the facilities of these languages instead.

14.3 Write and test a subroutine for perspective presentation and apply this to an object description derived from the Box or Extrude subroutines. Experiment with different eye distances and window sizes. Use rotations about each of the axis in turn. Show that, by rotating about the X-axis, vertical lines no longer appear vertical.

14.4 Write and test a Z-clipping routine based on the parametric method given in the text. Devise a version to deal with polylines. Note that the routine has to determine which end of a clipped line is visible. In a clipped polygon, sometimes the first point on the line will be visible and the second invisible; sometimes it will be the other way round. Remember too, that the clipped polygon can have more points in it than the unclipped one.

14.5 Try to devise a program to exploit all the 3-D methods given (including the painters' algorithm) in order to draw a number of objects in a scene. You will need a fast sorting routine to assist in properly using the painters' algorithm. The normal Bubblesort will be satisfactory for a small number of faces (say, up to 20) but, for a larger number, a sorting method such as Shellsort or Quicksort will be necessary.

14.6 Write a subroutine using Lambert's Law with ambient light correction to give you the colours to shade polygonal planes. Remember to apply the formula to each of the original R, G and B values and that there must be a maximum value which, no matter what the formula says, must not be exceeded. (Why?)

15

Putting It All Together

We now have sufficient information about graphics programming to put together a system that will let us make diagrams and drawings of 2-D and 3-D objects with reasonable ease. This will not have all the facilities that a professional graphics system might possess but will enable us to create and store drawings built up of lines either in colour or in monochrome and to edit these (during creation or at a later date). The drawings we make can be properly scaled to suit the output devices we have to hand. Curves, ellipses, circles and circular arcs can be accommodated and areas can be hatched in a variety of ways. If we have some graphics input device such as a mouse or digitiser, we can create the drawings interactively.

To facilitate the programming of such a system we can think of the subroutines we have created as grouped into six categories:

1 Subroutines to initialise the graphics system; for example, Set-window, Set-wsviewport and Makescales.
2 Subroutines to accept input and facilitate interaction; for example, Createlines and Menuchoice.
3 Subroutines to do 2-D and 3-D modelling; for example, Circle, Polyfit, Cubicfit and Extrude.
4 Subroutines to perform 2-D and 3-D transformations such as translations, rotations and scaling.
5 Subroutines to deal with data-structures; for example, Create-segment, Putdata, Getdata and Discop.
6 Subroutines to perform drawing tasks; for example, Drawline, Polyline, Hatch and Doros.

To make a comprehensive 2-D and 3-D drawing system, we must have subroutines from each of the categories. However, a minimal 2-D system could consist of the following:

Category 1:

Set-window	Table 10.4
Set-wsviewport	Table 10.5
Makescales	Table 10.6
Viewtrans	Table 10.7
Clippoly	Table 10.9
Intersect	Table 10.10
Visible	Table 10.11

Category 3:

Unitcircle	Table 8.3
Arc	Table 8.4
Twocirctan	Table 8.10

Category 4:

2-D transformations

Category 6:

Polyline	Table 11.3
Hatch	Table 11.5

Virtually all the figures in this book could have been drawn with a graphics system supporting only this small group of subroutines. Of course, it requires more manual effort to exploit a minimal system than it does with one having a fuller set of facilities. In one having no interactive capabilities, for example, all the data for our drawings would have to be worked out and entered into the subroutines by hand. However, you should start with just this minimal system and gradually add new subroutines as you feel the need for them. In this way you can have a working system after only a few hours coding. As time goes on, you will have incorporated not only the routines given here but also many of your own, particularly to model shapes like squares, rectangles, cubes and other regular 2-D and 3-D figures that you use a lot. In order not to have the system grow out of bounds, you may find it useful to have separate 2-D and 3-D systems and perhaps even special programs which create the object data independently of the drawings.

You will need to incorporate more tests for incorrect data and bad subroutine calls than we have shown in the outline subroutines and

algorithms of the text. In particular, whenever some of our subroutines detect an error, they call on the program to stop. (Set-
window and Set-wsviewport, for example, do this.) Safe though
such action might be, it is not very friendly and you will want to
invite your users to correct the error dynamically where possible
rather than bring the program to an emergency end. This will
especially be the case where drawings and other data can be entered
interactively.

Further Reading

As you progress with your system you will be able to use it not only to do drawings but also to test some of the new ideas in computer graphics techniques that are continually being developed. These are written about in detail in various specialist magazines. After working through this book you should have little difficulty in understanding what the technical papers in these journals are about.

There are three journal sources in particular that you should consult for the very latest thinking: *Computer Graphics Forum*, published by the European Association for Computer Graphics (Eurographics), and *Computer Graphics* and *Transactions on Computer Graphics*, published by the Special Interest Group on Computer Graphics of the Association for Computing Machinery (ACM SIGGRAPH). These publications are essential reading for anyone interested in developing their skills in this area. Membership of both these organisations, too, is available without special qualifications and they hold annual International Conferences: Eurographics, in various European cities; SIGGRAPH, around the USA. Back copies of the published proceedings of these conferences are enormously valuable sources. Many public libraries and most university and college libraries will stock copies of the journals and the proceedings. (Do not be afraid of going to one of these private libraries – the librarians there are invariably helpful and anxious to assist interested members of the public as well as students.)

Three books will also assist in the development of your computer graphics skills: *Principles of Interactive Computer Graphics* (Second Edition), by W. M. Newman and R. F. Sproull (McGraw-Hill Book Company, 1979); *Fundamentals of Interactive Computer Graphics* by J. D. Foley and A. van Dam (Addison-Wesley, 1982); and *Procedural Elements for Computer Graphics* by D. F. Rogers (McGraw-Hill Book Company, 1985). You can think of this book as an introductory text to all three of these although each has its different approach. Rogers's book is full of useful algorithms and worked examples which you can use to test the subroutines you will have written after working through this text. Fortuitously, Rogers also uses substantially the same pseudo-code as we have used here. (This, incidentally, is founded on a version of BASIC employed in the Tektronix 4054A desk-top computers.)

Computer graphics can only properly be learned by doing. Books and journals help, but you can only be sure you understand the principles by programming them and testing the results with all sorts of examples. It was Confucius who truly said:

I hear and I forget,
I see and I remember,
I do and I understand.

Appendix 1:

Vector and Matrix Algebra

Vectors are ordered sets of numbers which, in the context of our graphics work, can be used to represent lines having both a length and a direction. Although the numbers defining vectors (or *components* as they are called)

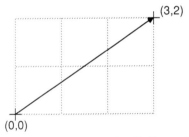

Figure A1.1   A vector from point $(0, 0)$ to point $(3, 2)$

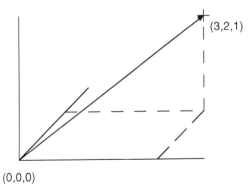

Figure A1.2   A vector from point $(0, 0, 0)$ to point $(3, 2, 1)$

can be made to represent a large variety of things, we use them here to indicate coordinates of position with respect to an orthogonal cartesian coordinate system as defined in Chapter 6. A vector such as (3,2) can be thought of as a representation of a line in 2-D space running from the origin of the coordinate system (0,0) to the point (3,2) as in Figure A1.1. Similarly, the vector (3,2,1) can be thought of as a line in 3-D space drawn from the origin (0,0,0) to the point (3,2,1) as in Figure A1.2.

Algebraic manipulation and arithmetic operations can be performed on vectors almost as if they were the usual form of numbers. They can, for example, be added or subtracted, multiplied by an ordinary number or multiplied by another vector. Division of vectors, on the other hand, is not possible.

Vector addition and subtraction

The vector (X1,Y1) can be added to the vector (X2,Y2) to give another, (X1 + X2,Y1 + Y2). The geometric effect of vector addition is shown in Figure A1.3 where A, represented by (3,2), is added to B, represented by (1,4), to produce C, represented by (4,6). You will see that the operation A + B is equivalent to drawing a line from the origin three units in the

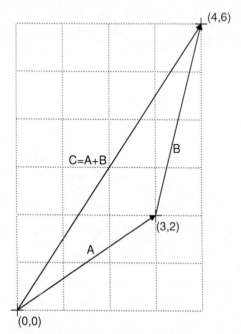

Figure A1.3 Vector addition

X-direction and two units in the Y-direction then drawing a line from this point, one unit in the X-direction and four units in the Y-direction. Furthermore, the operation $A + B$ arrives at the same point as the operation $B + A$.

$A - B$ gives us a vector $(X1 - X2, Y1 - Y2)$. The geometric effect of this is shown in Figure A1.4 where B, $(1,4)$ is subtracted from A, $(3,2)$ to produce $A - B$, $(2,-2)$. You will see that the operation $A - B$ is equivalent to drawing a line from the end of B to the end of A. As in normal arithmetic, unless $A = B$, the vector $A - B$ is not the same as the vector $B - A$. In fact, $A - B$ is the same length as $B - A$ but the lines they represent are drawn in opposite directions.

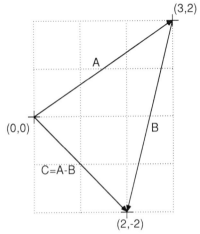

Figure A1.4   Vector subtraction

Scalar multiplication

When a vector is multiplied by a positive number, we change its length. Thus $S * (X,Y,Z)$ gives a new vector $(S * X, S * Y, S * Z)$. If S is in the range 0 to 1, the resultant vector gets smaller (or stays the same length if $S = 1$). If S is greater than 1, the vector gets larger. The same effects apply if S is negative but, in addition, the direction of the vector is reversed.

Vector length

The length of the vector $(X1,Y1)$ is given by the expression:

Length $= \sqrt{(X1^2 + Y1^2)}$

The length of $(X1,Y1,Z1)$ is given by:

Length $= \sqrt{(X1^2 + Y1^2 + Z1^2)}$

Thus length is calculated using the Theorem of Pythagoras.

Vector multiplication

Vectors can be multiplied together in two different ways. One of these ways is called the *inner* or *dot* product and is written as A·B (spoken of as 'A dot B'). A·B is a number which applies in 2-D or 3-D space (and spaces of higher dimension too, but these do not concern us here). The other is called the *vector* or *cross* product and is written as A × B (spoken of as 'A cross B'). A × B is a vector but this is undefined in 2-D space.

The dot product

If we have two non-zero vectors in 2-D or 3-D space, their dot product is defined as a real number given by:

A · B = Length (A) * Length (B) * Cos (Q)

Q being the angle between the lines.

With the vectors A: (XA,YA,ZA) and B: (XB,YB,ZB), neither of which is of zero length, the inner product is computed from the components of the vector by the expression:

A · B = XA * XB + YA * YB + ZA * ZB

To find the angle, Q, between two vectors, A and B, we have:

Cos (Q) = (A · B) / (Length (A) * Length (B))
      = (XA * XB + YA * YB + ZA * ZB) / L

where L = $\sqrt{((XA^2 + YA^2 + ZA^2) \cdot (XB^2 + YB^2 + ZB^2))}$.
As an example, if A = (3,−4,0) and B = (1,2,−2) then:

A · B = 3 − 8 + 0 = −5
Length (A) = 5
Length (B) = 3
Cos (Q) = −5 / (5 * 3) = − 1 / 3
Thus Q = 109.471 degrees

The angle in this case is measured in the plane formed by the two lines as indicated in Figure A1.5. If we wish to calculate the angle between two lines which start from a common point, P, other than the origin (as in Figure A1.6), we have to translate the start and endpoints of the lines to the origin before we make the dot product. Thus, if the start point of line 1 is P: (XP,YP,ZP) and the endpoint is (XA,YA,ZA) and, in addition, the start point of line 2 is P and the endpoint is (XB,YB,ZB), we must use the new vectors (XA–XP,YA–YP,ZA–ZP) and (XB–XP,YB–YP,ZB–ZP) in order to calculate the dot product.

If two non-zero vectors, A and B, have A · B = 0 then, because Cos(90) = 0, the lines A and B represented are *orthogonal* (at right angles) to one another. Orthogonality is illustrated in Figure 6.2.

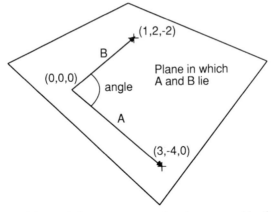

Figure A1.5   The angle between two vectors is measured in the plane in which they both lie

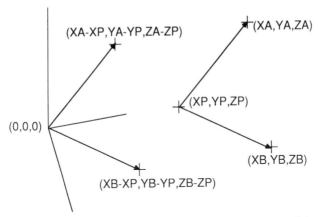

Figure A1.6   The dot product must be calculated at the origin

The vector product

The vector product, $A \times B$, defines another vector, C, which is orthogonal to both A and B. This means that $A \cdot C = 0$ and $B \cdot C = 0$.

If A is the vector (XA,YA,ZA) and B is (XB,YB,ZB), $A \times B$ is calculated from the expression:

$$C = A \times B = (XC,YC,ZC)$$

Where

XC = YA * ZB − ZA * YB
YC = ZA * XB − XA * ZB
ZC = XA * YB − YA * XB

As an example, if A = (5,−3,1) and B = (−1,−1,2),

C = A × B = (XC,YC,ZC)

and

XC = (−3 * 2) − (1 * −1) = −6 + 1 = −5
YC = (1 * −1) − (5 * 2) = −1 − 10 = −11
ZC = (5 * −1) − (−3 * −1) = −5 − 3 = −8

Therefore C = (−5,−11,−8) and this vector is at right angles to both A and B as we can check if we compute the dot products A · C and B · C.

A·C = XA * XC + YA * YC + ZA * ZC
    = (5 * −5) + (−3 * −11) + (1 * −8)
    = −25 + 33 − 8
    = 0
B · C = XB * XC + YB * YC + ZB * ZC
    = (−1 * −5) + (−1 * −11) + (2 * −8)
    = 5 + 11 − 16
    = 0

A plane surface is defined by any three separate points on it (which are not in one line) and, hence, by any two lines joining these points. For this reason, the property of orthogonality possessed by the vector product makes it of considerable importance in computer graphics where we frequently need to find vectors which are *normal* (another word for orthogonal) to a surface. Often, too, we need to make these normals of unit length. We do this by dividing each component by the total length of the normal. Thus, the normal (−3,−6,−2) has the length, L:

L = √(9 + 36 + 4) = 7

This means that the unit normal is (−3/7,−6/7,−2/7). Checking the length of this we see that:

Ln = √(9/49 + 36/49 + 4/49) = 1

Unlike the dot product, the vector product is dependent on the order in which the vectors are multiplied together. In other words, A × B is not the same as B × A. In fact, A × B = − (B × A) showing that A × B points in the opposite direction to B × A. You should check this with the vectors A = (5,−3,1) and B = (−1,−1,2) which we used above.

Appendix 2:

Using the Subroutines

For the reasons given in the Introduction, we have described our sub-routines in a pseudo-code which is not designed to run on a computer. You will be working in a language such as BASIC, Pascal or C and will need to convert the pseudo-code routines into that language. The routines are program modules which have the form:

Subroutine Name (Input parameters; Output parameters)
Body of the subroutine
End of subroutine

The input parameters are those which pass data to the routine and the output parameters are those which pass data from it to the rest of the program. The two groups of parameters are separated by a semicolon. Those readers who program only in standard BASIC will be unfamiliar with the conventions of passing data by means of parameters. They should note that the parameters are dummy variables which have names used only by the subroutine itself. Thus the subroutine Anglecalc (Table 8.8) has the dummy input variables XC, YC, X, Y, Flag and the dummy output variable, A. To use the subroutine, you give it the actual variable names (or constants, in the case of input parameters) that the rest of the program uses. If we include in our program the statement:

Call Anglecalc (Xstart, Ystart, Xend, Yend, 0; Specialangle),

the subroutine will use Xstart as XC, Ystart as YC, Xend as X, Yend as Y, 0 (the constant, zero) as Flag. It will also set Specialangle equal to the value of A that it calculates. The program is then free to use Specialangle as the angle in degrees between the horizontal and the line from (Xstart,Ystart) to (Xend,Yend). The advantage of this arrangement is, of course, that we can make many calls to the routine with all sorts of different parameter names without worrying – as we normally have to in BASIC – that we might be using a variable name that has already been assigned.

Inside the subroutines we distinguish between *local* and *global* variables.

220   Computer Graphics

We say that variables are *local* if they exist only in the subroutine: they are *global* if, when assigned, they affect variables of the same name outside the subroutine. We also distinguish between *integer* numbers (whole numbers) and *real* numbers (decimal numbers). BASIC does not normally require us to make this distinction – although many modern BASICs work more efficiently if we do. Typed languages such as Pascal and C, on the other hand, insist that variables are assigned to their correct categories before use.

Many versions of BASIC do not allow the use of dummy parameters so, in order for you to translate the subroutines to that language, you either have to assign different variable names throughout the subroutines (as is done in Table A2.1) or use a trick which is encapsulated in Table A2.2. The

Table A2.1

```
1 REM--test of polygon clipping routine in BASIC
10 W1 = 0: W2 = 1200: W3 = -600: W4 = 600
20 N = 3
30 DIM A1(N,2), O1(2*N,2), O2(2*N,2)
40 REM--read the polygon coordinates and assign then to O1()
50 FOR J = 1 TO N
60 READ A1(J,1), A1(J,2)
70 O1(J,1) = A1(J,1): O1(J,2) = A1(J,2)
80 NEXT J
90 DATA 600,1000,1400,800,1400,-600
95 REM--check each edge in turn
100 FOR E = 1 TO 4: GOSUB 1000: NEXT E
190 REM--print results
200 FOR J = 1 TO C-1: PRINT O2(J,1), O2(J,2): NEXT J
999 END
1000 REM--clip subroutine
1010 C = 1
1020 S1 = O1(N,1): S2 = O1(N,2)
1040 FOR J = 1 TO N
1050 P1 = O1(J,1): P2 = O1(J,2)
1070 X1 = P1: Y1 = P2: GOSUB 3000
1080 IF V = 1 THEN 1200
1090 X1 = S1: Y1 = S2: GOSUB 3000
1100 IF V = 1 THEN 1110
1105 GOTO 1400
1110 X1 = S1: Y1 = S2: X2 = P1: Y2 = P2: GOSUB 1500
1115 IF R > 1 OR R < 0 THEN 1400
1120 O2(C,1) = X: O2(C,2) = Y
1130 C = C + 1
1135 GOTO 1400
```

```
1200 X1 = S1: Y1 = S2: GOSUB 3000
1210 IF V=1 THEN 1300
1220 X1 = S1: Y1 = S2: X2 = P1: Y2 = P2: GOSUB 1500
1225 IF R > 1 OR R < 0 THEN 1250
1230 O2(C,1) = X: O2(C,2) = Y
1240 C = C +1
1250 O2(C,1) = P1: O2(C,2) = P2: C = C + 1
1270 GOTO 1400
1300 O2(C,1) = P1: O2(C,2) = P2: C = C + 1
1400 S1 = P1: S2 = P2
1410 NEXT J
1420 FOR J = 1 TO C - 1
1430 O1(J,1) = O2(J,1): O1(J,2) = O2(J,2)
1450 NEXT J
1455 N = C - 1
1460 RETURN
1500 REM--intersect subroutine
1510 ON E GOTO 2000,2200,2400,2600
2000 R = (W4 - Y1) / (Y2 - Y1)
2010 X = X1 + (X2 - X1) * R
2020 Y = W4
2030 RETURN
2200 R = (W2 - X1) / (X2 - X1)
2210 Y = Y1 + (Y2 - Y1) * R
2220 X = W2
2230 RETURN
2400 R = (W3 - Y1) / (Y2 - Y1)
2410 X = X1 + (X2 - X1) * R
2420 Y = W3
2430 RETURN
2600 R = (W1 - X1) / (X2 - X1)
2610 Y = Y1 + (Y2 - Y1) * R
2620 X = W1
2630 RETURN
3000 REM--visibility subroutine
3010 ON E GOTO 3020,3040,3060,3080
3020 X0 = W1: Y0 = W4: X9 = W2: Y9 = W4
3030 GOTO 3090
3040 X0 = W2: Y0 = W4: X9 = W2: Y9 = W3
3050 GOTO 3090
3060 X0 = W2: Y0 = W3: X9 = W1: Y9 = W3
3070 GOTO 3090
3080 X0 = W1: Y0 = W3: X9 = W1: Y9 = W4
```

```
3090 V1 = (X9 - X0) * (Y9 - Y1) - (Y9 - Y0) * (X9 - X1)
3100 V = 1
3110 IF V1 <= 0 THEN V = 0
3120 RETURN
```

Table A2.2

```
100 REM--a program illustrating how to handle subroutine calls
105 REM--subroutine is of form: MOCK(J;A) ie, it accepts J and returns A
110 DIM T(5),T$(5)
120 B$ = "string1"
130 A = 10.4
140 FOR J = 1 TO 2
150 A = A * J
160 REM--prepare to call subroutine by storing program values
170 T(1) = A: T(2) = J: T$(1) = B$
180 PRINT "In program: A = ";A;"J = "; J;"B$ = ";B$
190 REM--call subroutine MOCK which uses own values of these variables
200 GOSUB 1000
210 PRINT "Returned value of A = ";A
220 REM--revert to the original values
230 A = T(1): J = T(2): B$ = T$(1)
240 NEXT J
250 END
1000 REM--SUBROUTINE MOCK(J;A)
1010 B$ ="string2"
1020 J = J * 2
1030 A = J + 2
1040 PRINT "In MOCK : A = ";A;"J = ";J;"B$ = ";B$
1050 RETURN
```

```
In program: A =   10.4 J =   1 B$ = string1
In MOCK : A =   4 J =   2 B$ = string2
Returned value of A =   4
In program: A =   20.8 J =   2 B$ = string1
In MOCK : A =   6 J =   4 B$ = string2
Returned value of A =   6
```

Printout from the program

idea is to keep aside a special set of array variables, say, T() and T$(), which store the values of any main program variables having the same names as those in the subroutine. After leaving the subroutine, the return variables are assigned new names and the others are given their original values again. If you code the example in Table A2.2, and assign different values to the variables, you will see how the trick works and soon learn how to use it in your programs.

Another construction which is not used in BASIC is the Case statement. In the way that we have used it, too, it is slightly different from the usage in C. Our Case statement takes the form:

Case of num:
    1:X = 5
    2:X = 26.5
    3:X = −14
End of case

Here, the program performs its actions depending on the value of num. If num = 1, X is set to 5 and control passes to the statement after the **End** of case; if num = 2, X is set to 26.5 and control passes to the statement after the **End** of case; if num = 3, X is set to −14 and control passes on. This idea is easily programmed in BASIC using the computed GOTO construct if that is available, otherwise, the ordinary GOTO. For example:

```
150 IF NUM = 1 THEN X = 5: GOTO 200
160 IF NUM = 2 THEN X = 26.5: GOTO 200
170 X = −14
200 REM--REST OF PROGRAM
```

Table A2.3 shows how Case might be used in a Pascal program.

Table A2.3

```
program rotmattest; { part of a Pascal test of the rotmat subroutine }
type
  mat4by4 = array[1..4, 1..4] of real;
var
  i : integer;
  a : real;
  mat : mat4by4;
  procedure rotmat (axstr : char; a : real; var mtrx : mat4by4);
{ to make a 4 x 4 rotation matrix }
  var
   c, s : real;
   i, j : integer;
begin
  a := a * 3.1415926 / 180; { convert angle to radians }
  c := cos(a);
```

```
                    s := sin(a);
                    for i := 1 to 4 do
                     for j := 1 to 4 do
                     begin
                      if i = j then
                       mtrx[i, j] := 1
                      else
                       mtrx[i, j] := 0
                     end;
                    case axstr of
                     'x' : begin
                          mtrx[2, 2] := c;
                          mtrx[2, 3] := -s;
                          mtrx[3, 2] := s;
                          mtrx[3, 3] := c;
                         end; { of x-axis rotation case }
                     'y' : begin
                          mtrx[1, 1] := c;
                          mtrx[1, 3] := s;
                          mtrx[3, 1] := -s;
                          mtrx[3, 3] := c;
                         end; { of y-axis rotation case }
                     'z' : begin
                          mtrx[1, 1] := c;
                          mtrx[1, 2] := s;
                          mtrx[2, 1] := -s;
                          mtrx[2, 2] := c;
                         end; { of z-axis rotation case }
                    end; { of case }
                   end; { of rotmat subroutine }
```

Table A2.4 gives an example of an Apple Macintosh program in Microsoft BASIC. It tests a Sweep subroutine based on the ideas outlined in Chapter 13 and illustrates how some of the different subroutines we have created can be used in a practical situation.

Table A2.4

```
'Macintosh MS BASIC program to create an object by rotational
'sweeping and to view it in perspective. The profile must be described
'in the positive x-y plane with first point at the top (note that
'the Macintosh has its origin at the top left corner)

'set up screen and find centre
  w1 = 0: w2 = 0: w3 = 511: w4 = 341
```

```
    w5% = INT(w3/2): w6% = INT(w4/2)      'centre of screen
    WINDOW 1,,(w1,w2)-(w3,w4),3    'a Macintosh command

'make declarations and set up some constants
    DIM Px(18), Py(18), FPx(256), FPy(256), FPz(256)
    DIM Poly(40), sqfaces(480,5), trifaces(48,4), XP(256), YP(256)
    pi=3.1415926#
    f=pi/180                              'radian correction factor
    dist = 250                            'eye distance for viewing

'read profile data and number of faces
    READ numfaces%                        'total number of faces
    READ numpts%                          'total number of points
    IF numpts% > 20 THEN PRINT "Sorry not more than 20 points allowed":
STOP
    READ PSx, PSy                             'the top point
    FOR J% = 1 TO numpts%-2        'the intermediate points
       READ Px(J%), Py(J%)
    NEXT J%
    READ PEx, PEy                             'the bottom point

'set up all the points
    FPx(1) = PSx: FPy(1) = PSy: FPz(1) = 0            'top point
    FOR J% = 2 TO numpts%-1                   ' first slice
       FPx(J%) = Px(J% - 1): FPy(J%) = Py(J% - 1): FPz(J%) = 0
    NEXT J%
    currnum% = numpts%
    angle = 360/numfaces%*f               'change angle to radians
    FOR K% = 1 TO numfaces%               'all the other slices
       FOR J% = 2 TO numpts% -1
          FPx(currnum%) = INT(Px(J% - 1)* COS(K% * angle))
          FPy(currnum%) = Py(J% -1)
          FPz(currnum%) = INT(Px(J% - 1) * SIN(K% * angle))
          currnum% = currnum% + 1
       NEXT J%
    NEXT K%
       FPx(currnum%) = PEx: FPy(currnum%) = PEy: FPz(currnum%) = 0
       last% = currnum%                      'all points complete

    'set up all the face lists
    'top triangular faces
    FOR facenum% = 1 TO numfaces%
       pt1% = 2 + (facenum% - 1) * (numpts% - 2)
```

```
      pt2% = 2 + facenum% * (numpts% - 2)
      trifaces(facenum%, 1) = pt1%
      trifaces(facenum%, 2) = 1
      trifaces(facenum%, 3) = pt2%
      trifaces(facenum%, 4) = pt1%
   NEXT facenum%
   'bottom triangular faces
   FOR facenum% = 1 TO numfaces%
      pt1% = (numpts% - 1) + (facenum% - 1) * (numpts% - 2)
      pt2% = (numpts% - 1) + facenum% * (numpts% - 2)
      currnum% = facenum% + numfaces%
      trifaces(currnum%, 1) = pt1%
      trifaces(currnum%, 2) = pt2%
      trifaces(currnum%, 3) = last%
      trifaces(currnum%, 4) = pt1%
   NEXT facenum%
   numtrifaces% = currnum%
   'all square faces
   sqfacenum% = 0
   FOR side% = 0 TO numfaces% -1
      FOR layer% = 1 TO numpts% - 3
         sqfacenum% = sqfacenum% + 1
         start% = (layer% +1) + (numpts% - 2) * side%
         sqfaces(sqfacenum%, 1) = start%
         sqfaces(sqfacenum%, 2) = start% + (numpts% - 2)
         sqfaces(sqfacenum%, 3) = start% + (numpts% - 2) +1
         sqfaces(sqfacenum%, 4) = start% + 1
         sqfaces(sqfacenum%, 5) = start%
      NEXT layer%
   NEXT side%                          'all facelist completed
   numsqfaces% = sqfacenum%
   'put all points into perspective with eye at (0, 0, -dist)
   'and translate to see on screen
   FOR J% = 1 TO last%
      perspfactor = dist / (FPz(J%) + dist)
      XP(J%) = INT(FPx(J%) * perspfactor + .5) + w5%
      YP(J%) = INT(FPy(J%) * perspfactor + .5) + w6% - 100
   NEXT J%

   'draw all triangular faces
   FOR J% = 1 TO numtrifaces%
      num% = trifaces (J%,1)
      CALL MOVETO (XP(num%), YP(num%))
```

```
   FOR K% = 2 TO 4
      num% = trifaces(J%,K%)
      CALL LINETO (XP(num%),YP(num%))
   NEXT K%
NEXT J%
'draw all square faces
FOR J% = 1 TO numsqfaces%
   num% = sqfaces (J%,1)
   CALL MOVETO (XP(num%), YP(num%))
   FOR K% = 2 TO 5
      num% = sqfaces(J%,K%)
      CALL LINETO (XP(num%),YP(num%))
   NEXT K%
NEXT J%

hold:IF INKEY$="" THEN hold    'keep picture on screen until <return> pressed
END

DATA 8,7
DATA 0,200, 20,200,  20,140, 40,120, 40,60, 20,40, 0,40
```

Index

232 *Computer Graphics*